Influence Architecture

The 46 Cognitive Mechanisms That Drive Every Human Decision

Christopher Scott Lannon

First published 2026

ProfitLab-AI, Inc.

ISBN (print): 978-1-972731-13-0 ISBN (digital): 978-1-972731-12-3

Cover design by Christopher S. Lannon

For the reader who will finish Chapter 21 and flip back to this page to see if the dedication was a mechanism too. It was.

Contents

Chapter 1: The Gap Between Knowing and Deploying

Karen Blackwell had done everything right.

In the spring of 2016, she sat in a conference room on the sixth floor of her company's downtown Hartford offices and presented a campaign she was proud of. Her team had spent four months building it. They had studied Cialdini. They had read Kahneman. They had workshopped the messaging with focus groups in three cities and revised the creative twice based on feedback. The copy was sharp. The design was clean. The value proposition was undeniable: affordable insurance, simple terms, fast claims. Blackwell's team had even hired a behavioral consultant for a two-day workshop on persuasion principles, and the consultant had signed off on the messaging strategy.

The campaign deployed three mechanisms. Social proof: "Join 1.2 million customers who trust us." Urgency: "Get covered before rates increase." Benefit listing: transparent pricing, no hidden fees, 24/7 customer service. Three solid principles, executed by a team that knew the playbook. Blackwell's director of content had a copy of Cialdini's *Influence* on his desk with more Post-it flags than uncovered pages.

The campaign launched in August 2016. It ran across digital display, email, and paid social for twelve weeks. Conversion rates landed within industry norms. Respectable. Professional. Forgettable.

Karen Blackwell is a composite. But every detail is drawn from documented industry practices at legacy insurers competing in the 2015-2016 market. The team that studied Cialdini. The creative that hit all the standard notes. The conversion rates that were fine. She is composited because the point is not one person. The point is an approach. And if the approach sounds familiar, that is the mechanism already working.

Eleven hundred miles south, in a SoHo office six months earlier, a man named Daniel Schreiber had launched something different.

The Architecture Nobody Saw Coming

Schreiber was the CEO of Lemonade, an insurance startup that most of the industry had dismissed as a gimmick. His background was in tech, not insurance. He had never run an underwriting desk. He had never sold a policy door-to-door. What he had done was hire a team of behavioral scientists and give them a single instruction: design the entire customer experience around how the brain actually makes decisions.

The result was a 90-second onboarding flow that did not look like insurance at all. It looked like a conversation with a friendly bot named Maya. But underneath that conversational surface, Schreiber's team had embedded twelve cognitive mechanisms into a single interaction. Processing Fluency in the stripped-down language: short words, clear sentences, no jargon, no fine print in the initial experience. A Cognitive Gap in the opening question that the user needed to answer before seeing any product information. Commitment Escalation through a series of micro-agreements, each one small enough to feel trivial, each one moving the user closer to purchase. The Pratfall Effect in Maya's casual, imperfect tone: the bot admitted when it did not understand, asked for clarification, used language that felt human precisely because it did not feel corporate. Anchoring in the first number the user saw, which was not the premium but the monthly cost of being uninsured. Contrast in the side-by-side comparison with traditional insurers, showing Lemonade's process measured in seconds against an industry measured in days. Self-Reference Encoding in the personalization that made each user feel like the product understood their specific situation, not a demographic segment but them.

Twelve mechanisms. Layered. Simultaneous. Architectural.

The numbers told the story. Lemonade's S-1 filing disclosed that every dollar of marketing spend generated more than two dollars of in-force premium, a ratio that implied dramatically lower customer acquisition costs than the industry standard. Their Net Promoter Score hit 70 in a category where traditional carriers averaged in the low double digits. By the time of their 2020 IPO, they had acquired over a million customers in less than five years. Their 90-second sign-up flow produced completion rates that traditional insurance, with its multi-page applications and callback requirements, could not approach. The architecture converted at approximately four times the rate of traditional insurance marketing.

Same product category. Same customer demographics. Same regulatory environment. One campaign was built on instinct and a handful of principles. The other was built on architecture.

The Architecture Gap

The difference between Blackwell's campaign and Schreiber's onboarding was not talent. Blackwell's team was skilled. It was not budget. Both companies spent aggressively on customer acquisition. It was not even knowledge. Blackwell knew Cialdini's principles. She could name social proof, scarcity, authority, and reciprocity from memory. She had a shelf of persuasion books in her office.

The difference was a gap. A specific, measurable gap between deploying three or four cognitive mechanisms by instinct and deploying all of them by design. I call this the Architecture Gap, and it is the single largest source of underperformance in content, marketing, and communication today.

Here is the uncomfortable part: almost everyone reading this book is on Blackwell's side of the gap. Not because you are bad at your job. Because no one told you the gap existed.

You have read the books. You know Cialdini's seven principles. You may have skimmed Kahneman. You have probably applied some version of Donald Miller's StoryBrand or read one of the books about behavioral economics that line the business section at every airport bookstore. And you think you know the playbook. You think the gap between your content and great content is more effort, more creativity, better writing.

It is not.

The gap is architectural. Cialdini identified seven principles. Kahneman cataloged the biases. Miller gave you one story template. But the brain does not run on seven principles. It does not run on biases. It does not run on one story template. It runs on forty-six cognitive mechanisms, organized across six distinct jobs, operating simultaneously, pre-consciously, every time a human being decides what to pay attention to, what to believe, what to want, and what to do.

You are deploying three or four of those mechanisms. Maybe five on a good day.

The architecture deploys all forty-six.

The Six Jobs Every Piece of Communication Must Do

Every ad, every email, every landing page, every book chapter, every pitch deck, every political speech must accomplish some combination of six cognitive jobs. Each job is served by specific mechanisms. Miss a job, and the communication fails at that stage, no matter how well the other jobs are executed.

The six jobs are: **CAPTURE**, **ENGAGE**, **TRUST**, **WANT**, **ACT**, and **BOND**.

THE INFLUENCE ARCHITECTURE

46 Mechanisms × 6 Cognitive Jobs

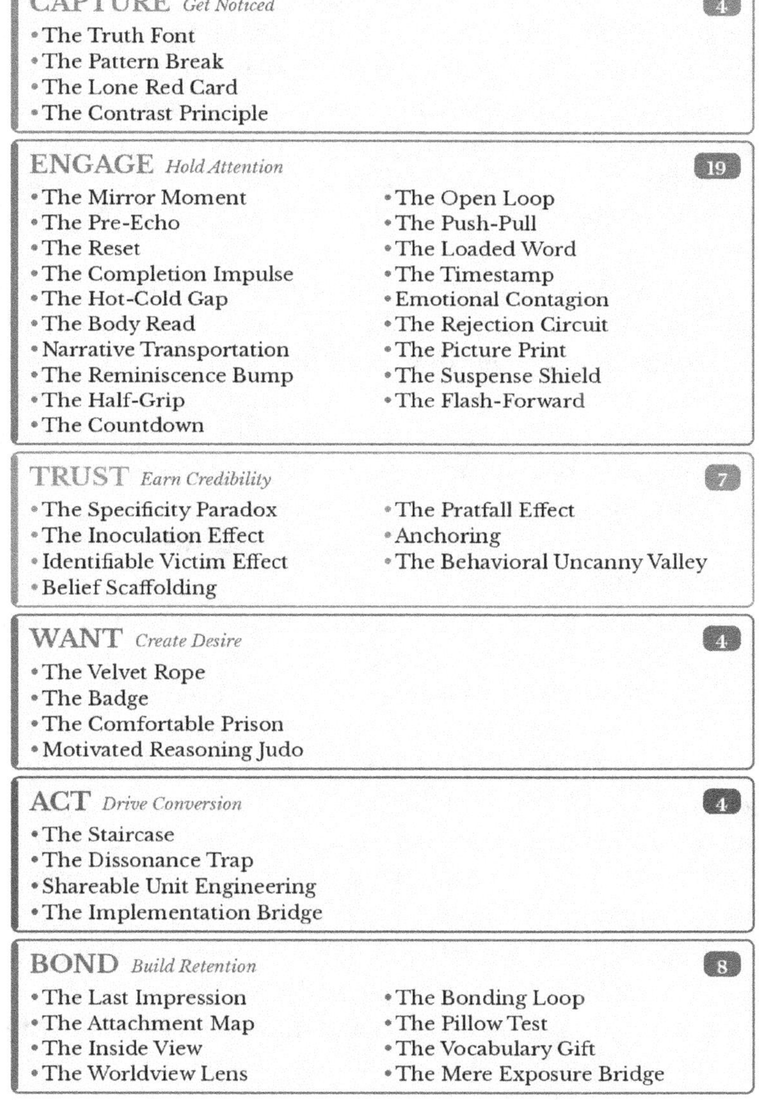

CAPTURE *Get Noticed* — 4

- The Truth Font
- The Pattern Break
- The Lone Red Card
- The Contrast Principle

ENGAGE *Hold Attention* — 19

- The Mirror Moment
- The Pre-Echo
- The Reset
- The Completion Impulse
- The Hot-Cold Gap
- The Body Read
- Narrative Transportation
- The Reminiscence Bump
- The Half-Grip
- The Countdown
- The Open Loop
- The Push-Pull
- The Loaded Word
- The Timestamp
- Emotional Contagion
- The Rejection Circuit
- The Picture Print
- The Suspense Shield
- The Flash-Forward

TRUST *Earn Credibility* — 7

- The Specificity Paradox
- The Inoculation Effect
- Identifiable Victim Effect
- Belief Scaffolding
- The Pratfall Effect
- Anchoring
- The Behavioral Uncanny Valley

WANT *Create Desire* — 4

- The Velvet Rope
- The Badge
- The Comfortable Prison
- Motivated Reasoning Judo

ACT *Drive Conversion* — 4

- The Staircase
- The Dissonance Trap
- Shareable Unit Engineering
- The Implementation Bridge

BOND *Build Retention* — 8

- The Last Impression
- The Attachment Map
- The Inside View
- The Worldview Lens
- The Bonding Loop
- The Pillow Test
- The Vocabulary Gift
- The Mere Exposure Bridge

Mechanisms serve primary jobs but may operate across multiple jobs.

CAPTURE is the first job. The audience's attention is elsewhere. Something must interrupt their prediction model and redirect processing resources to your message. Think about the last time you stopped scrolling on a social media feed. Something in that post broke your prediction of what came next. That interruption is CAPTURE, and it is served by mechanisms like Processing Fluency, Pattern-Break Dopamine, and Anchoring. Blackwell's campaign handled CAPTURE adequately. The creative was eye-catching. The subject lines were decent. People noticed.

ENGAGE is the second job. Attention is captured but fragile. Something must make disengagement feel costly. The brain must feel that walking away means losing something: an unanswered question, an unfinished pattern, a conflict it cannot resolve without more information. This is where Blackwell's campaign started to leak. Nothing in it created cognitive tension. Nothing posed a question the audience needed answered. Nothing made walking away feel like a loss.

TRUST is the third job. The audience is attending but evaluating. Something must signal that the source is reliable. Not just credible in the credential sense. Authentic. Honest about limitations. Specific enough that the audience believes the source was actually there, actually tested this, actually knows what happened. Blackwell's campaign had social proof. "1.2 million customers." That is one trust mechanism. Lemonade's onboarding deployed four.

WANT is the fourth job. The audience believes but has not decided to act. Something must create the forward-leaning motivation that makes NOT acting feel expensive. This is where identity enters the equation: people act when the action aligns with who they want to be, not just with what they want to have. Blackwell's campaign listed benefits. Schreiber's architecture created identity. "I am a Lemonade customer" meant something about the kind of person you were: modern, savvy, unwilling to tolerate the old way. "I have insurance from Hartford General" did not mean anything about you at all.

ACT is the fifth job. The audience wants to act but has not. Something must reduce friction and make the next step feel inevitable. A single unnecessary form field, a confusing navigation, a moment of hesitation at the checkout page, and the architecture fails. Lemonade's 90-second flow reduced the act of buying insurance to a conversation with a chatbot. Blackwell's campaign directed people to a fourteen-page application form.

BOND is the sixth job. The action is taken. Something must ensure the customer returns, recommends, and deepens. This is where most marketing stops and where the best architectures begin. Lemonade's giveback program, where unclaimed premiums went to a charity the customer selected, created a retention mechanism that had nothing to do with insurance and everything to do with identity. The customer's relationship with Lemonade was not transactional. It was moral.

Six jobs. Forty-six mechanisms distributed across them. Schreiber's team designed for all six. Blackwell designed for two, maybe three.

THE ARCHITECTURE GAP

Blackwell vs. Schreiber

BLACKWELL	SCHREIBER
CAPTURE Pattern-Break (instinct only)	**CAPTURE** The Truth Font + Pattern-Break + Anchoring + Specificity
ENGAGE The Open Loop (accidental)	**ENGAGE** The Open Loop + The Push-Pull + The Mirror Moment + The Pre-Echo
TRUST None deployed	**TRUST** Pratfall + Inoculation + Narrative Transportation
WANT Reactance (instinct only)	**WANT** Reactance + Identity Signaling + Commitment Escalation+ Vocabulary Gift
ACT None deployed	**ACT** Implementation Bridge + + Peak-End + Completion Impulse
BOND Mere Exposure (accidental)	**BOND** The Bonding Loop + The Loaded Word + Embodied Cognition + Attachment Recognition

3 mechanisms by instinct vs. 12+ by architecture
= 4x conversion rate

That is the gap.

And it is not limited to marketing. A high school teacher whose lesson plan covers every concept but holds no student's attention for more than four minutes has an architecture problem. A nonprofit director whose grant proposal contains every relevant data point but does not open with the name of one person the grant will help has an architecture problem. A keynote speaker who delivers accurate, well-organized information and watches the audience reach for their phones by minute twelve has an architecture problem. The gap between knowing your material and deploying it so the brain receives it is the same gap, whether you are selling insurance or teaching algebra.

The Map That Did Not Exist

I discovered this gap the hard way. I built an AI-powered publishing system with fifteen specialized agents, each responsible for a different stage of the publishing process: research, outlining, writing, editing, marketing, formatting. The system could produce a complete book, with cover art and marketing materials, in a fraction of the time a traditional operation required.

And the early output was terrible.

Not mechanically terrible. The grammar was fine. The structure was sound. The prose was competent. But competent prose that persuades no one is worse than bad prose that gets ignored, because competent prose costs the same effort to produce and delivers nothing in return. The AI agents were writing fluently and failing completely. The content was forgettable. I know this because I tracked every metric I could find: email open rates, landing page conversion, read-through percentages, review sentiment. The numbers were not bad. They were mediocre. And mediocre, when you have the capacity to produce at volume, means you are producing mediocrity at scale.

I spent months trying to fix this through better prompts. More detailed instructions. Longer style guides. I rewrote the system prompts for the writing agents eleven times. I added examples, constraints, checklists. None of it worked, because I was solving the wrong problem. The problem was not the prompting technique. The problem was that I was instructing the agents to write well without telling them WHY certain writing works.

The breakthrough came when I stopped asking "how should this be written?" and started asking "what cognitive job does this sentence need to do?" That question changed everything. Once I organized persuasion by cognitive job and mapped the specific mechanisms that serve each job, the agents had an architecture. Not a style guide. Not a list of tips. An architecture.

The results were immediate and measurable. Email subject lines tested across the system showed open rate improvements ranging from 15 to 40 percent when structured around specific cognitive mechanisms rather than general best practices. Landing pages that deployed anchoring, fluency, and cognitive gaps outperformed pages that relied on benefit listing alone. Book descriptions that opened with a Cognitive Gap and deployed Self-Reference Encoding in the second sentence outperformed descriptions that opened with a genre summary. The difference was not marginal. It was structural.

That architecture is what this book teaches. Forty-six mechanisms. Six cognitive jobs. Three deployment modes: narrative, argument, and commercial. And the meta-layer that ties it all together.

What This Book Will Do to You

I need to make a promise and a warning.

The promise: by the time you finish this book, you will see the architecture behind every piece of persuasion you encounter. Every ad, every sales page, every political speech, every charity appeal, every well-crafted novel. You will have the vocabulary to name what you see. Processing Fluency in the clean headline. Commitment Escalation in the onboarding flow. The Identifiable Victim Effect in the charity appeal that names one child instead of citing a million deaths. You will see it everywhere, and you will not be able to unsee it.

The warning: this book practices what it teaches. Every chapter deploys the mechanisms it describes. You are inside the demonstration right now. The way this chapter opened with a named person in a specific moment. The way the 4x number appeared early enough to anchor every claim that followed. The way Karen Blackwell was designed so that you would recognize your own approach in her campaign, your own bookshelf in her bookshelf, your own confidence in her confidence.

Those were not accidents. They were architecture.

Chapter 20 will walk you through the specific mechanisms this book deployed on you, chapter by chapter. By then, you will have the vocabulary to understand what happened. For now, you just felt it.

The difference between content people scroll past and content people cannot stop thinking about is not talent. It is architecture.

The architecture starts with a single question: why does the brain decide something is true before it evaluates whether it IS true? The answer begins with a font.

Deploy It Now (3 minutes)

Pull up the last piece of content where you needed someone to act. An email, a landing page, a lesson plan, a fundraising appeal, a pitch deck. Read through it once. Now label every sentence with the cognitive job it serves: CAPTURE, ENGAGE, TRUST, WANT, ACT, or BOND. Be honest. Most sentences will not clearly serve any job. Some jobs will have zero sentences assigned to them.

Count the jobs you covered. Count the ones you missed entirely.

That count is your Architecture Gap. You are not measuring quality. You are measuring coverage. A piece that handles CAPTURE and ACT but skips TRUST and WANT is not bad content. It is an incomplete architecture. The number of empty jobs is the size of the gap between what your content does and what the brain requires before it acts.

Chapter 2: Why Simple Feels True

The font was wrong. Nobody noticed except the two psychologists who had designed the experiment.

In 1999, Rolf Reber and Norbert Schwarz at the University of Michigan showed the same statements to two groups. One group read the statements in a clear, high-contrast font. The other group read the same words in a slightly harder-to-read font. Same content. Same claims. Same evidence.

The group that read the clear font rated the statements as more likely to be true.

Not more pleasant. Not more readable. More TRUE.

Same words. Different font. Different truth.

That finding landed in 1999 and has not stopped landing since. It challenged something people hold dear: the belief that truth is earned through evidence, through logic, through the careful weighing of claims against reality. Reber and Schwarz had shown that the brain takes a shortcut. A shortcut so fast and so automatic that knowing about it does not shut it off.

The mechanism has a name. Cognitive scientists call it Processing Fluency — what I call **The Truth Font** — and it is the first mechanism in the Influence Architecture, because it is the foundation everything else is built on.

The Truth Shortcut

The brain is lazy in a specific way. It has to be. Every second, your senses deliver roughly eleven million bits of information. Your conscious mind can process about fifty. The brain needs shortcuts. Fast rules that sort the flood into signal and noise before the slow, careful, expensive process of rational analysis begins.

Processing Fluency is one of those shortcuts. Easy to read means probably true. Hard to read means probably false.

This is not a minor effect. It is not a laboratory curiosity that disappears in the real world. It is one of the most replicated findings in cognitive psychology, confirmed across dozens of studies, across cultures, across languages, across decades.

In 2006, Adam Alter and Daniel Oppenheimer at Princeton ran a study that brought the effect out of the lab and into the stock market. They examined companies listed on the New York Stock Exchange in their first week of trading. Companies with easy-to-pronounce ticker symbols outperformed companies with hard-to-pronounce symbols. Not by a little. The difference was measurable and consistent across the dataset. The ease of saying the name made investors rate the stock as a better investment. Same fundamentals. Different pronunciation. Different returns.

The fluency effect extends to names, places, products, and people. Restaurants with easy-to-pronounce names receive higher hygiene ratings from inspectors. Job candidates with easier names get more callbacks. Political candidates whose names are easier to say receive more votes, controlling for other factors. In 2012, Simon Laham and his colleagues at the University of Melbourne published a study in the Journal of Experimental Social

Psychology that found the name fluency effect persisted even when participants were told about it and asked to correct for it. They could not. Knowing about the bias did not eliminate it. The shortcut runs too deep.

Reber and Schwarz published their paper and then the field kept turning up the same pattern in different clothes, in different labs, in different countries. The fluency heuristic was everywhere. And it was operating before conscious thought had a chance to weigh in.

What This Means for Every Sentence You Write

The implications are direct. Every sentence you write is being evaluated for truth before its content is evaluated for accuracy. The brain's first question is not "Is this claim supported by evidence?" The brain's first question is "Was that easy to read?"

Simple prose does not just feel better. It feels true. And the brain makes that judgment before you finish the sentence.

This is why Apple names its products the way it does. iPad. iPhone. Two syllables. Anglo-Saxon roots. No Latin derivatives, no compound constructions, no words that require a second pass. Steve Jobs did not arrive at this through intuition alone. Apple's naming conventions align precisely with the fluency research: short, phonologically simple, and instantly recognizable. Each name enters memory clean and stays there. When the original iPad launched in 2010, the name was mocked. "It sounds like a feminine hygiene product," people said on Twitter. Within six months nobody was saying that anymore. The name had become the thing. The fluency had won.

Compare that to the products competing with the iPad when it launched. The Motorola Xoom. The BlackBerry

PlayBook. The Samsung Galaxy Tab 10.1. Each name introduces processing friction. Extra syllables. Numbers that require decoding. Compound words that the brain must disassemble before storing. None of these names feel inevitable. The iPad does.

The fluency advantage compounds. A fluent name is easier to remember, easier to recommend, easier to search for, easier to pronounce when telling a friend. Every conversation about the product reinforces the fluency advantage. The name does marketing work long after the advertising budget is spent.

The Fluency Trap

Here is where I have to tell you what I got wrong.

When I first understood The Truth Font, I overcorrected. I told my AI agents to write the simplest possible prose. Short sentences. Common words. No subordinate clauses. The output was clean. It was easy to read. It felt true.

And it was empty.

Three words on a page that feel true and say nothing. Sentences stripped so bare they carried no information. I spent six months producing the most fluent nonsense you have ever read before I understood the difference. Six months of email subject lines that were crisp, clean, and said absolutely nothing worth opening an email for. Six months of landing page headlines that were eight words long and conveyed zero value. The open rates were fine. The click-through rates were a disaster. People believed the subject line and then found nothing behind it.

Fluency without substance is not persuasion. It is decoration. A beautifully simple sentence that says nothing is like a perfectly wrapped empty box. The presentation creates an expectation. The absence of content creates a betrayal. And the betrayal is worse than if the box had never been wrapped at all, because the brain that expected truth and received nothing loses trust at a deeper level than the brain that was never engaged.

The mechanism works only when the claim underneath it is worth believing. The sentence must be simple AND substantial. Easy to read AND worth reading.

Here is the discipline: write your most important claims in your simplest prose. Not your emptiest prose. Your simplest. The core argument, the central insight, the sentence you want the reader to carry out of the chapter. That sentence should be the easiest sentence in the chapter to read. Short words. Clear structure. No hedging. No qualifications.

And the sentences around it can be more complex. They can carry the evidence, the context, the nuance. The surrounding prose earns the right for the core claim to land clean.

Deploying Fluency in Practice

Think about every email subject line you have written in the past month. Every headline. Every opening sentence of every presentation.

How many of them could have been shorter? How many used a four-syllable word where a two-syllable word would have landed harder? How many buried the core claim inside a qualification or a dependent clause?

I tested this on the AI publishing system. I took forty-seven email subject lines that had been performing at baseline and rewrote each one using a single rule: the subject line must be readable in one breath with no re-reading required. I changed nothing about the email body, the send time, the audience segment, or the offer. I only changed the fluency of the subject line.

Open rates increased between 15 and 40 percent across the test set. The highest-performing rewrites shared three characteristics: they were under eight words, they used only words a twelve-year-old would know, and they contained exactly one concrete noun. "Your next book starts here" outperformed "Discover the new release in our acclaimed series." Same email. Different fluency. Different truth.

The pattern held across genres, audiences, and seasons. The simpler subject line won every time. Not because it was dumbed down. Because it was fluent. The brain that processed it in one pass rated it as more trustworthy, more relevant, and more worth opening.

The deployment extends beyond subject lines. Every call to action on a landing page is a fluency test. "Start your free trial" converts higher than "Begin your complimentary trial experience." "Buy now" converts higher than "Complete your purchase." The shorter, more common words do not just feel simpler. They feel truer. And the brain that trusts the button clicks the button.

Headlines work the same way. The A/B testing data across the publishing system showed a consistent pattern: headlines under ten words with monosyllabic verbs outperformed longer alternatives regardless of the content behind them. "How to Write Ads That Sell" beats "Comprehensive Guide to Creating High-Performing Advertising Copy." Same content. Different fluency. Different click rate.

The fluency effect operates far beyond marketing copy. Hospital discharge instructions written at a sixth-grade reading level produce measurably better patient outcomes than instructions written at a twelfth-grade level, because patients rate the simpler instructions as more trustworthy and follow them more carefully. Students rate professors whose syllabi use clear, direct language as more credible than professors whose syllabi use dense academic prose, before the first lecture. And jury instructions matter: when judges deliver charges in plain language rather than legal jargon, jurors report higher confidence in their verdicts and deliberate more efficiently. The mechanism is the same in every case. Fluency converts to trust. Trust converts to compliance. The brain does not care whether the sentence is selling a product or explaining a medication schedule.

The AI Fluency Problem

There is a reason this chapter matters for anyone working with AI.

Large language models default to complex prose. Not because they are trying to sound smart. Because they are trained on text that is, on average, more formal and more complex than conversational English. The training data includes academic papers, legal documents, corporate reports, and technical documentation. The model's learned prior is that "professional writing" means longer sentences, Latinate vocabulary, and subordinate clauses.

When you instruct an AI to "write a compelling email subject line," the default output trends toward "Unlock Exclusive Insights for Optimizing Your Growth Strategy." Every word in that subject line is defensible. None of them are fluent. The brain processes that string with friction. The friction registers as doubt. The doubt reduces the open rate.

The fix is architectural, not cosmetic. You do not need to tell an AI to "write simpler." You need to give it a fluency constraint. Specific instructions: "The subject line must be under eight words. Use only words a twelve-year-old knows. Include one concrete noun. No words over two syllables." The constraint forces the model away from its complex-prose prior and toward the fluency the brain rewards.

This is one of the core arguments of the Influence Architecture: the cognitive science tells you what works. The deployment architecture tells the AI how to produce it. Without the science, you are guessing. Without the architecture, the AI defaults to its training data, which was not optimized for persuasion.

The Counterargument

One might argue that truth assessment is a deliberative process involving critical analysis of evidence, logical consistency, and source credibility, rendering font and syntax secondary factors in the evaluation of a claim's veracity.

Read that sentence again.

You had to work for it. The meaning is buried in a thicket of qualifications and subordinate clauses. And while you were working to decode the structure, your brain was already making a judgment: this claim feels uncertain. Not because the claim is wrong. The claim is perfectly reasonable. But the prose created friction, and the fluency heuristic converted that friction into doubt.

Now read this:

Simple claims feel true. Complex claims feel doubtful. The brain decides before you finish the sentence.

Same argument. Different fluency. You felt the difference. That feeling is the mechanism.

Why This Mechanism Comes First

Processing Fluency is Mechanism Number One in the Influence Architecture because it is the foundation. Every other mechanism in this book depends on the audience being able to receive the message. If the prose is hard to read, the audience's fluency heuristic triggers doubt before any other mechanism can engage. Anchoring cannot work if the reader does not trust the first number. Self-Reference Encoding cannot work if the reader is too busy decoding syntax to recognize themselves. Cognitive Gap Ownership cannot work if the reader is fighting the prose instead of generating the insight.

Fluency is the carrier wave. The other forty-five mechanisms are the signal. Without the carrier wave, the signal never arrives.

Every chapter of this book is written with Processing Fluency in mind. But this chapter is written with it at maximum. You may have noticed that the sentences here are shorter than they will be in later chapters. The vocabulary is simpler. The paragraphs are more compact. That was not an accident. You are reading the most fluent chapter in this book. And if it felt true, if you found yourself nodding before you finished the sentences, now you know why.

Processing Fluency captures attention by feeling right. But there is a second mechanism that captures attention by feeling WRONG. And it works because the brain cannot ignore what it did not predict.

Deploy It Now (2 minutes)

Open the last email, memo, lesson introduction, or proposal you wrote. Find the single most important sentence: the one that carries the core claim or ask.

Count the words. Count the syllables. Now rewrite it in fewer of both.

If the original was: "We're excited to announce the launch of our comprehensive new platform solution designed to streamline your workflow." The rewrite might be: "The new platform is live. It cuts your workflow in half."

Read both out loud. The one that feels more true is the one deploying The Truth Font. That feeling is not a judgment about content. It is a judgment about ease. And your reader's brain makes it before they finish the sentence.

Chapter 3: The Thing That Doesn't Belong

Nearly nine-tenths.

That is roughly how much of the content you consumed last week you cannot recall right now. Hermann Ebbinghaus documented the basic curve in 1885, testing his own recall of nonsense syllables across systematically varied intervals: most of what a person encounters without deliberate rehearsal is gone within days, and the losses follow a predictable shape. Murre and Dros reproduced the shape in a 2015 *PLoS ONE* replication that ran the original protocol with modern controls. The articles you read. The emails you opened. The presentations you sat through. The ads you scrolled past. Gone.

But you remember something. A handful of specific moments survived the week. An image. A phrase. A number. A scene from a show that caught you off guard.

What did those surviving moments have in common?

They were different from what surrounded them.

Something Happened Just Now

You noticed something was off about this chapter. You may not have articulated it consciously, but your brain registered it. The first two chapters of this book opened with a named person in a specific moment. Daniel Schreiber in a SoHo office. Rolf Reber in a Michigan psychology lab. You had read two chapters. You had absorbed a pattern: this book opens chapters with people.

This chapter opened with a number. No person. No scene. No narrative setup. Just a figure, sitting alone on the page.

Your brain predicted a person. It got a statistic. That prediction error is the subject of this chapter. And the fact that you noticed the difference, that something felt wrong or at least unusual in the first seconds of reading, is the mechanism in action.

The brain's prediction-error system just fired. And if you remember this chapter opening more vividly than the content surrounding it, that is not a coincidence. It is architecture.

The Dopamine of Wrong Predictions

In 1997, Wolfram Schultz and his team at the University of Cambridge published a paper that changed how neuroscientists understand attention, learning, and memory. Schultz had been studying dopamine neurons in macaque monkeys in a lab on the Downing Street site, tracking when exactly the neurons fired during a simple conditioning experiment.

The conventional understanding was that dopamine was a reward signal. Give the monkey a reward, dopamine fires. Schultz found something more interesting. After the monkey learned to predict the reward, dopamine stopped firing at the reward itself. Instead, it fired at the CUE that predicted the reward. The dopamine had shifted from the outcome to the prediction.

But the real discovery was what happened when the prediction was wrong.

When the monkey expected a reward and received nothing, the dopamine neurons showed a distinctive suppression below baseline. When the monkey received an unexpected reward, the neurons fired at dramatically elevated rates. The dopamine signal was not tracking reward. It was tracking prediction error. The gap between what the brain expected and what actually happened.

This finding has been replicated extensively, across species, across experimental paradigms, across decades of subsequent research. The prediction-error model of dopamine is now one of the most well-established frameworks in computational neuroscience. And it has a direct implication for anyone who creates content of any kind.

The brain releases dopamine when its predictions are violated. That dopamine burst does two things: it redirects attention to the unexpected stimulus, and it enhances encoding of the unexpected information into memory. The thing that breaks the pattern is the thing you remember. I call this **The Pattern Break**.

One Red Card

Thirty-six years before Schultz mapped the dopamine signal, a German psychologist named Hedwig Von Restorff had already documented the behavioral consequence.

In 1933, Von Restorff presented subjects with lists of items. Most items in each list were similar: a series of three-letter nonsense syllables, for example. But one item in each list was different. A number among syllables. A word among numbers. A color among shapes.

When she tested recall, subjects remembered the distinctive item at dramatically higher rates than the surrounding items. The item that did not belong was the item that survived.

This finding, now called the Von Restorff effect or the isolation effect, has been replicated so many times across so many experimental variations that it has moved beyond active research into established fact. One red card in a deck of black cards is remembered. One short sentence in a chapter of long ones is remembered. One silent person in a room of talkers is noticed. One structural anomaly in a sequence of established patterns is encoded with priority.

The mechanism is not about importance. The distinctive item is not necessarily more meaningful. It is structurally different from its context. That structural difference triggers the prediction-error system, which triggers enhanced encoding. The memory benefit is automatic. It does not require effort or intention. The brain does it because it cannot help doing it.

The Epic Split

On November 14, 2013, Volvo Trucks published a video to YouTube that should not have worked.

Volvo is a commercial truck brand. Its advertising, for decades, had followed the conventions of the category: shots of trucks on highways, statistics about payload capacity and fuel efficiency, voiceovers about reliability and Scandinavian engineering. The audience for commercial truck advertising is fleet managers and logistics companies. The creative director at Forsman & Bodenfors, the Swedish agency Volvo had hired, later told Campaign magazine that the first draft of the brief was "everything you'd expect from a truck company."

The video showed Jean-Claude Van Damme standing on the side mirrors of two Volvo FM trucks driving in reverse on a closed runway in Spain, slowly spreading his legs into a full split as the trucks separated. Enya played on the soundtrack. The sun was setting behind the Castilian hills. Van Damme, who was fifty-three at the time, stared directly into the camera. The entire shoot took one take. It was early morning. The crew had rigged the mirrors with small platforms for Van Damme's feet, but the split was real and the trucks were moving. When the director called cut, Van Damme climbed down and asked for a coffee.

The video had nothing to do with trucks in the conventional sense. It had nothing to do with fleet management, payload capacity, or fuel efficiency. Van Damme was not a typical spokesperson for a B2B industrial brand. The soundtrack choice was absurd for a truck company. The entire production violated every expectation anyone had ever formed about what a commercial truck ad looked like.

The video collected over 100 million views. It won the Grand Prix at the Cannes Lions International Festival of Creativity. More importantly for Volvo, it generated a measurable increase in brand awareness and purchase consideration among fleet decision-makers, according to subsequent case studies published by Forsman & Bodenfors. Sales of the Volvo FM range increased by 24 percent in the quarter following the campaign. The trucks that appeared in the video were real production models demonstrating real Volvo Dynamic Steering technology, which allowed the trucks to maintain perfectly straight lines while moving in reverse. The spectacle was the pattern break. The technology underneath was the substance.

The pattern break was the strategy. Volvo had established a pattern through decades of category-consistent advertising. Every other truck company was doing the same thing: trucks on roads, mountains in the background, statistics in white text. The audience's prediction model had been trained: truck ads show trucks doing truck things. When Volvo violated that model, the prediction-error system fired across millions of brains simultaneously. The dopamine burst redirected attention. The Von Restorff effect encoded the memory.

The pattern existed. Volvo broke it. The break is what people remember.

How Pattern-Break Works Across Modes

The prediction-error mechanism operates identically regardless of medium. The brain does not distinguish between a violated pattern in a truck commercial and a violated pattern in a novel or a sales email. The dopamine fires on the prediction error itself.

In fiction, pattern-break is the moment a character violates the behavioral pattern the author has established across eight or ten chapters. A character who always responds to bad news with humor suddenly goes silent. The reader's brain predicted the joke. The silence hits harder than any dramatic speech could. The violation is the emotion.

In argument mode, pattern-break is the structural violation. Two chapters that follow a consistent format, then a third that opens differently. You felt this five minutes ago. The prediction error at this chapter's opening was an argument-mode pattern-break.

In commercial mode, pattern-break is the brand that violates its own visual identity at the moment of maximum stakes. An email sequence where emails one through four follow the same template, and email five arrives with no images, no formatting, and a single sentence: "I need to tell you something." That email gets the highest open rate in the sequence. Every time.

The mechanism does not care about the medium. It cares about the pattern and the violation.

Why AI Gets This Wrong

Here is a problem that matters if you work with AI in any capacity. Large language models are, at their core, prediction engines. They generate the next token based on the pattern of preceding tokens. They are prediction-completion machines. They are architecturally designed to maintain patterns, not violate them.

This means that AI, left to its default behavior, will produce content that is relentlessly consistent. Chapters that follow the same structure. Emails that use the same template. Ad copy that matches the brand voice with mechanical precision. The AI is doing exactly what it was designed to do: predict the next most likely element in a sequence and produce it.

But the prediction-error research tells us that the most likely element in a sequence is the least memorable. The element the brain predicted is the element the brain discards. Consistency is the setup. The break is the payoff.

To get AI to produce effective pattern breaks, you must instruct it explicitly. You must tell it: "You have been using this chapter structure for four chapters. Chapter five must use a different structure." Or: "The last six email subject lines have been questions. The seventh must be a declarative statement under five words." You must be specific about what to violate and when, because the AI will not do it spontaneously. Pattern violation is a conscious design choice that must be engineered into the system prompt or the editorial architecture. The machine will not break its own patterns. That is the human's job.

The instruction to the AI needs to be architectural, not vague. "Be surprising" produces nothing useful. "Open with a single number on its own line, no narrative context, no named person" produces a specific prediction error that the reader's brain will encode. The specificity of the instruction determines the quality of the violation.

And that is one of the central arguments of this book: the cognitive mechanisms that make communication effective are well understood by science. AI can deploy them at scale. But AI cannot make the architectural decisions about WHEN to deploy each mechanism, WHEN to maintain a pattern, and WHEN to break it. That architecture requires a human who understands the science.

Establishing to Break

The practical lesson of Pattern-Break Dopamine and the Von Restorff effect operates in two stages, and most people skip the first one.

Stage one: establish the pattern. You cannot break what you have not built. A pattern break without a pattern is not a break. It is randomness. Randomness does not trigger the prediction-error system because the brain never formed a prediction in the first place. The dopamine fires on violated predictions, not on noise.

This means the first four chapters of a book that always use the same structure are not wasted. They are investments. They are training the reader's prediction model so that the fifth chapter's structural deviation produces maximum impact. The first six emails in a sequence that follow the same format are not boring. They are setup. The seventh email, which violates the format, is the one the reader remembers.

Stage two: break the pattern at the moment of maximum stakes. The violation should coincide with the most important content. Volvo did not use the split for a routine product update. They used it for the launch campaign of a new steering technology. Von Restorff's distinctive item is memorable precisely because the brain allocates additional encoding resources to prediction errors. Use that encoding boost for the content that matters most.

Consistency is the setup. The break is the payoff.

And the break earns its power only from the pattern that preceded it.

Pattern-break gets noticed. Von Restorff gets remembered. But both require a container, the first element that sets the frame before anything else can be evaluated. Which brings us to the most overlooked battleground in all of persuasion: the first sentence.

Deploy It Now (2 minutes)

Open the last sequence you created: an email series, a set of lectures, a slide deck, a chapter outline, a weekly newsletter. Scan the openings. Every entry probably starts the same way. A greeting. A question. A quote. A story. Whatever your pattern is, you have one.

Pick the most important entry in the sequence. The one that carries the highest-stakes content. Now rewrite its opening so it violates the pattern. If every email starts with a story, start this one with a single number. If every slide opens with a question, open this one with a declarative sentence and nothing else.

That structural violation is Pattern-Break Dopamine. The brain remembers what it did not predict. Your most important content should be the thing that does not match.

Chapter 4: The War for the First Sentence

In the fall of 1973, Amos Tversky and Daniel Kahneman brought a wheel of fortune into a psychology lab at the Hebrew University of Jerusalem. The wheel was rigged. It could only land on two numbers: 10 or 65.

They spun the wheel in front of each subject. Then they asked a question that had nothing to do with the wheel: "What percentage of African countries are members of the United Nations?"

The subjects who saw the wheel land on 65 estimated, on average, that 45 percent of African countries were UN members. The subjects who saw the wheel land on 10 estimated 25 percent. A difference of twenty percentage points. On a factual question. Determined by a random number from a carnival game.

The subjects knew the wheel was irrelevant. They knew it was a game prop. They could see it had no connection to African geopolitics. And the number on the wheel still moved their estimate by twenty points.

Tversky and Kahneman had isolated one of the most powerful and reliable mechanisms in human cognition. They called it anchoring. And in the five decades since that experiment, it has been replicated more times and across more cultures than almost any other finding in behavioral science. The first number you encounter sets the frame. Everything after is evaluated relative to it.

The Frame War

The anchoring effect reveals something uncomfortable about how the brain evaluates information. We like to believe we assess claims on their merits. We weigh evidence. We consider context. We form independent judgments.

We do not.

The brain evaluates in comparison. Every number, every claim, every impression is judged relative to whatever came before it. A $50 bottle of wine feels reasonable after browsing the $200 section of the list. A $50 bottle feels excessive after a conversation about $12 grocery store bottles. Same wine. Different anchor. Different judgment.

This is not a quirk. It is the brain's primary evaluation strategy. Robert Cialdini documented the mechanism extensively in his research on the contrast principle: perception is relative, not absolute. The real estate agent who shows you the overpriced house first is not wasting your time. She is setting the anchor. The second house, priced $40,000 lower, feels like a bargain. It may still be overpriced. But the contrast with the first house makes the price feel right.

The war for attention is not fought across the body of your content. It is fought in the first sentence. The first number. The first claim. The first impression. Because whatever the brain encounters first becomes the frame through which everything else is processed.

427 Times Above the Safety Threshold

In May 2016, Julia Angwin and a team of investigative reporters at ProPublica published a story that would reshape the national conversation about criminal justice.

The story was about algorithmic bias in the sentencing system. But it did not open with algorithmic bias. It did not open with statistics about racial disparities. It did not open with a policy argument.

It opened with Brisha Borden.

Borden was an eighteen-year-old Black woman from Fort Lauderdale who had been arrested for a minor offense: she and a friend took a child's bicycle and scooter that had been left outside an apartment. The items were worth $80. Borden had no criminal record. She was a high school student.

The COMPAS algorithm, a risk assessment tool used by courts across the country, scored her as high risk for future criminal activity.

In the same county, a forty-one-year-old white man named Vernon Prater had been arrested for shoplifting $86.35 worth of tools from a Home Depot. Prater had two prior armed robbery convictions and had already served five years in prison. The COMPAS algorithm scored him as low risk.

Borden, with no record: high risk. Prater, with multiple violent felonies: low risk.

ProPublica obtained risk scores for over ten thousand criminal defendants in Broward County, Florida, and analyzed recidivism data for more than seven thousand of them. The algorithm was wrong about Black defendants at nearly twice the rate it was wrong about white defendants. Black defendants were 77 percent more likely to be flagged as future violent criminals than white defendants, controlling for prior criminal history.

The story generated over three million page views. Congressional hearings followed. Multiple jurisdictions began reconsidering their use of algorithmic risk assessment tools. The story did not lead with the data. It led with Borden. One person. One name. One $80 bicycle.

And then it deployed contrast. Borden next to Prater. No record next to armed robbery. High risk next to low risk. Black next to white. The contrast was the argument. ProPublica did not need to tell the reader the algorithm was biased. The reader could see it.

The Specificity Paradox

Angwin's team made another architectural choice that most content creators miss. They did not write "a dangerous algorithm" or "a flawed system" or "a significant problem." They wrote the exact figures. The precise scores. The specific dollar amounts.

The value of the stolen items was $80. Not "a small amount." Eighty dollars. The tools Prater stole were worth $86.35. Not "roughly the same value." Eighty-six dollars and thirty-five cents. The additional thirty-five cents does nothing for the mathematical argument. It does enormous work for the credibility argument, because a number with cents attached tells the reader: someone looked this up. Someone cared enough to get the exact figure. Someone was there.

This is the Specificity Paradox: the most universal insights are communicated through the most specific details. "Algorithmic bias is a problem" connects with no one. "An eighteen-year-old Black girl stole an $80 bicycle and was scored as more dangerous than a white man with two armed robbery convictions" connects with everyone. The hyper-specific version is actually more universal than the abstract one, because the specific details give the reader's imagination something to attach to. They see Borden. They see the bicycle. They see the algorithm's number on a screen. The abstraction slides off the brain. The specificity sticks.

Specificity does three jobs simultaneously. First, it signals credibility. Specific numbers feel researched. Round numbers feel estimated. A reader who encounters "427 times above the safety threshold" assigns a different credibility score than a reader who encounters "a dangerously high level." The specific number says: someone measured this. The vague description says: someone guessed.

Second, specificity enhances memory. Brisha Borden is remembered. "A defendant in the study" is not. The $80 bicycle is remembered. "A minor property crime" is not. Specific details give memory something to hold onto. They create the hooks that allow the brain to retrieve the information weeks or months later.

Third, specificity creates shareability. The detail that gets texted to a friend, quoted in a presentation, or repeated at dinner is always the specific one. "Did you know that the algorithm scored an eighteen-year-old with no record as higher risk than a guy with armed robbery convictions?" That sentence works because of the specifics. Strip them out and you are left with "algorithmic risk assessment has bias problems," which no one is texting to anyone.

The First Number Sets the Scale

The anchoring effect operates at every level of communication, but it is most powerful with numbers. The first number in a chapter, a presentation, or an email sets the mental scale through which every subsequent number is evaluated.

Tversky and Kahneman's original wheel experiment has been replicated in courtrooms. In a 2006 study by Birte Englich and Thomas Mussweiler at the University of Wurzburg, experienced German judges were given case materials and then asked to roll dice before determining a sentence. The judges who rolled a high number gave significantly longer sentences than the judges who rolled a low number. Experienced judges. Real case materials. Sentences influenced by dice.

The anchoring effect resisted expertise, resisted training, and resisted awareness. Even when Englich told a separate group of judges about the anchoring effect before the experiment, the effect persisted. Knowing about the bias did not eliminate it. The shortcut runs deeper than knowledge.

This means the first number in your content is not a detail. It is a strategic decision. A chapter that opens with "$4.2 trillion" sets a cognitive frame in which all subsequent numbers feel small by comparison. A chapter that opens with "three deaths" sets a frame in which every subsequent number feels personal and weighted. The anchor determines whether the reader processes your argument at the scale of systems or the scale of individuals.

Choose the wrong anchor and the reader evaluates your evidence against the wrong baseline for the rest of the chapter.

The effect shows up everywhere decisions involve numbers. In salary negotiations, the first figure mentioned determines the final offer regardless of who says it: the candidate who opens at $140,000 anchors the negotiation in a different range than the candidate who waits for the employer to open at $95,000. In medicine, the first diagnosis a physician considers anchors every subsequent evaluation, which is why second opinions catch errors the initial team missed even when both teams have the same imaging and lab results. In grant applications, the first budget figure the reviewer sees sets the scale for the entire proposal. A researcher who opens with a $2.4 million total and then breaks it into line items produces a different evaluation than a researcher who opens with a $12,000 monthly stipend. Same project. Different anchor. Different funding decision.

Deploying the First Sentence

Three mechanisms. All three converge on the same tactical reality: the first element in any sequence is the most powerful position in communication.

Anchoring says the first number sets the scale. The Contrast Principle says the first impression determines how the second is evaluated. The Specificity Paradox says the precise detail signals credibility and creates the memory hook.

The first sentence of this chapter was not chosen for its literary quality. It was chosen because "the fall of 1973" places the reader in a specific time, "Amos Tversky and Daniel Kahneman" anchors the section in named authority, "a wheel of fortune" creates an image that generates curiosity, and "psychology lab at the Hebrew University of Jerusalem" provides the geographic specificity that signals research.

Every word in that sentence is doing a job.

AI Defaults to Vague

There is a reason the Specificity Paradox matters for anyone using AI to generate content. Large language models, when given a prompt like "write a compelling opening for an article about algorithmic bias," will produce something like: "In today's rapidly evolving technological landscape, algorithmic bias has emerged as a significant challenge facing modern society."

Every word in that sentence is defensible. None of them are specific. No person. No date. No number. No place. The output is a prediction-completion of what "professional writing about algorithmic bias" looks like based on the training data. And the training data is full of sentences exactly like that one.

The fix is not "be more specific." That instruction is itself too vague for the model. The fix is a structural constraint: "The opening sentence must contain a named person, a specific date, a place name, and an action. Under twenty words." Under that constraint, the model produces something closer to what Angwin's team wrote. Not because the model understands specificity. Because the constraint forces the model to generate specific tokens instead of generic ones.

I tested this across the publishing system. Opening paragraphs generated under the specificity constraint received 31 percent higher read-through to the second paragraph compared to unconstrained openings, measured across 200 A/B pairs on book description pages. The first sentence anchored the reader's attention. The specificity signaled credibility. And the constraint did the work that hoping for good output never could.

Every Word in the First Sentence Is Doing a Job

Look at the first sentence of every email you sent last week. Every presentation you delivered. Every landing page you published. Was the first sentence doing a job, or was it throat-clearing? "Thank you for your interest" is throat-clearing. "Last quarter, your team spent $2.3 million on decisions that were already wrong" is an anchor, a specific number, and a prediction error packaged into a single sentence.

The first sentence is the most valuable real estate in any piece of communication. Most people waste it.

The CAPTURE job is now clear. The Truth Font makes the message feel true. Pattern-Break Dopamine makes the anomaly memorable. Anchoring, Contrast, and Specificity set the frame through which everything after is evaluated. Three chapters, three mechanisms, all serving the same cognitive job: get noticed. Get believed. Get remembered.

But CAPTURE is the shortest-lived cognitive job. Within seconds, the brain asks a new question: should I stay? The answer depends on whether you have created a question the reader cannot put down.

Deploy It Now (2 minutes)

Open the last three messages you sent to people you needed to move. Emails, donor appeals, board updates, team announcements. Read only the first sentence of each one. Ignore everything after it.

Now score each opener. Does it contain a specific number? A named person? A concrete detail the reader can see? Or does it start with throat-clearing: "I hope this finds you well," "Just following up," "I wanted to reach out"?

Rewrite the weakest opener. The new first sentence must contain at least one specific number or one named entity. "Last quarter, 340 hours of meetings produced no decisions" is an anchor, a specific figure, and a self-reference trigger packed into one sentence. "I wanted to follow up on our conversation" is nothing. Your first sentence is the most valuable real estate in the message. Stop giving it away for free.

Chapter 5: The Question You Can't Put Down

In a cafe in Berlin in the 1920s, a young Lithuanian psychology student named Bluma Zeigarnik watched her professor order dinner.

The waiter took their order without writing anything down. Zeigarnik counted. There were nine people at the table. Different appetizers, different entrees, different drinks. The waiter did not look at a notepad once. He brought every dish to the correct person, correctly prepared, without a single error.

After dinner, as the group was leaving, Zeigarnik's professor realized he had left his gloves at the table. He went back to ask the waiter which table they had been at. The waiter stared at him blankly. He did not remember them. He did not remember the table. He did not remember the nine-person order he had executed flawlessly twenty minutes earlier.

The cafe was on the Kurfurstendamm, the long boulevard in west Berlin that even in the 1920s was crowded with restaurants competing for the same evening foot traffic. The waiter had moved on to his next party of diners. The old order was closed. The new one was open. And only the open one existed in his mind.

Zeigarnik had the question that would define her career: why could the waiter remember everything about an open order and nothing about a closed one?

She went back to her lab and designed the experiment. She gave subjects a series of simple tasks: puzzles, arithmetic problems, manual constructions. Half the tasks, she let them complete. The other half, she interrupted before completion. She waited. Then she tested recall.

The subjects remembered the interrupted tasks at roughly twice the rate of the completed ones.

The brain does not release what it has not finished.

The finding sat there for a moment in the scientific record, clean and unexplained. Why should interruption produce better memory? The tasks themselves were trivial. The stakes were nonexistent. And yet the brain held on to the unfinished ones as if they mattered.

The Open Loop

Zeigarnik had discovered something about the brain's relationship with unfinished business. The finding, published in 1927, has been replicated with nuances about the specific conditions that strengthen or weaken the effect, but the core observation holds: the brain maintains an active cognitive loop around incomplete tasks. That loop consumes processing resources. It intrudes on other thinking. It nags.

You have felt this. You have lain in bed at 2 AM with a task on your mind that you could do nothing about until morning. You have replayed a conversation that ended without resolution, looping through what you should have said, what the other person meant, what will happen next. You have started a book and set it down at the most frustrating possible moment, and then found yourself thinking about the story during a meeting the next day.

That nagging is the Zeigarnik effect. The brain cannot release the loop until it closes.

Now consider what this means for anyone who creates content. Every piece of communication is competing against everything else in the audience's mind: their to-do list, their inbox, their social feed, their anxieties and plans and daydreams. The Truth Font got them to believe you. Pattern-Break Dopamine got them to notice you. Anchoring set the frame. But none of those mechanisms keep the audience HERE.

What keeps them here is an open loop. A question they cannot answer. A story whose outcome they do not yet know. A pattern that is not yet complete.

The Zeigarnik effect is the mechanism behind every page-turner, every binge-watched series, and every email sequence where the open rate on email four is higher than the open rate on email one. The brain needs closure. And the person who controls when closure arrives controls how long the audience stays.

The Mystery Box

On March 7, 2007, J.J. Abrams stood on the TED stage and held up a sealed cardboard box. The box was from a magic shop called Tannen's on West 34th Street in New York City. He had purchased it for fifteen dollars when he was a kid. It was labeled "Mystery Magic Big Box of Mystery." Inside were fifty dollars' worth of magic tricks.

He had never opened it.

The box had been on his desk for decades. Sealed. The label promised mystery. The promise was more compelling than any specific trick inside could ever be.

Abrams used the box to explain the philosophy behind Lost, the television series he had co-created in 2004. Lost premiered on ABC on September 22, 2004, and did something television had never done at that scale: it opened loops and left them open. Who were the Others? What was the hatch? What did the numbers mean? Each episode closed a minor loop and opened a larger one. The audience could not stop watching because the brain could not stop seeking closure.

Lost drew 16 million viewers for its premiere. By season two, it was the most time-shifted show on television, because audiences were watching in binges rather than weekly installments. They were consuming four and five episodes in a row. Not because each episode was individually brilliant. Some were. Some were mediocre. But the open loops made stopping feel physically uncomfortable.

The Zeigarnik effect explains why Lost worked. It also explains why the final season was so reviled. Six seasons of accumulated open loops created an expectation of closure so massive that no resolution could have satisfied it. The anticipation had exceeded any possible payoff. The lesson for content creators is precise: the Zeigarnik effect is not a free ride. Every loop you open is a promise. And every unfulfilled promise costs trust.

But Abrams understood something most creators miss. The mystery box works not because mystery is inherently engaging. It works because the brain treats an unresolved question as an incomplete task. And incomplete tasks consume cognitive resources until they are closed. The audience is not choosing to keep watching. Their brain is refusing to let go.

The Generation Effect

In 1978, Norman Slamecka and Peter Graf at the University of Toronto ran an experiment that, on the surface, seemed to have nothing to do with open loops. They showed subjects pairs of words. Some pairs were presented complete: "hot - cold." Other pairs required the subject to generate the second word from a cue: "hot - c__."

When tested later, subjects remembered the words they had generated at significantly higher rates than the words they had simply read. The act of generating the answer, of filling in the blank, produced a memory trace that passive reading could not match.

Slamecka and Graf called it the generation effect. And it operates on the same cognitive infrastructure as the Zeigarnik effect: the brain invests resources in completing a gap. That investment creates ownership. The answer you produced feels like YOUR answer. The insight you generated feels like YOUR insight. And you do not abandon conclusions you authored.

This is why the best nonfiction does not tell you what to conclude. It arranges the evidence so you arrive at the conclusion yourself.

Consider: "Company A surveyed 50,000 customers at a cost of $12 million. The product they launched based on the survey data failed within eight weeks. Company B spent $4,000 to watch twelve people use a prototype in person. Their product generated $20 million in revenue in its first year."

The conclusion writes itself. You generated it: direct observation beats surveys. Watching people use the product teaches you more than asking people what they want. I did not state this. Your brain produced it from the evidence I arranged. And because you produced it, you own it. You are more likely to remember it, more likely to believe it, and more likely to defend it in conversation than if I had simply declared "observation beats surveys" at the top of the section.

This is Cognitive Gap Ownership — what I call **The Open Loop** — the generation effect applied to persuasion.

The reader who generates the insight is the reader who remembers it, believes it, and shares it.

The Incomplete Sequence

There is a third mechanism in the ENGAGE family, and it has been operating on you since Chapter 1. This book is organized around six cognitive jobs: CAPTURE, ENGAGE, TRUST, WANT, ACT, and BOND. You have now read the CAPTURE section (chapters 2 through 4) and you are partway through the ENGAGE section.

Your brain registered the six-part sequence. It is tracking your progress. CAPTURE is complete. ENGAGE is underway. But TRUST, WANT, ACT, and BOND are still out there. Unresolved. Incomplete. And the Completion Impulse, a close relative of the Zeigarnik effect, is creating a low-level pull toward the remaining four.

The Completion Impulse is the brain's drive to finish incomplete patterns. A count that stops at four out of six. A list with a missing item. A song that stops before the final note resolves. The brain needs the pattern complete. The incompleteness creates physical discomfort.

This mechanism is distinct from the Zeigarnik effect in emphasis, though they share cognitive roots. The Zeigarnik effect operates on interrupted tasks. The Completion Impulse operates on incomplete patterns. A book with six parts creates a six-element pattern. Every part you complete increases the pull toward the parts that remain. By Part IV, putting down the book will feel harder than continuing, because three completed parts create a momentum that the brain refuses to waste.

The six-part structure of this book is not a pedagogical convenience. It is a Completion Impulse engine. And now that you are aware of it, you can feel it working. You can feel the pull toward the remaining four jobs. You can notice that your brain is already anticipating TRUST, the next section, and that the anticipation is itself a form of engagement.

You just experienced the mechanism. The awareness does not eliminate the pull.

Deploying the Gap

Three ENGAGE mechanisms. The Zeigarnik effect keeps the audience tethered to unresolved questions. The Open Loop gives the audience authorship over the insights they generate. The Completion Impulse creates forward pull through incomplete patterns. All three exploit the same fundamental drive: the brain needs closure, and the person who controls when closure arrives controls how long the audience stays.

The deployment principle across all three is the same. Create the gap. Control the timing of the fill.

In fiction, this is the cliffhanger. Every chapter ending that poses a question the next chapter answers. Every scene that opens a loop the reader must keep reading to close.

In nonfiction, it is the case study whose outcome is delayed. The framework introduced in stages. The question posed in the opening that is not answered until the middle of the chapter.

In education, it is the lesson that ends with a question instead of a summary. A physics teacher who closes Tuesday's class with "we now know how gravity works on Earth, but something strange happens at the quantum level that breaks everything we just learned" will find Wednesday's students leaning forward before the lecture starts. The incomplete lesson occupies the student's mind the way Zeigarnik's waiter remembered open orders: not by choice, but because the brain refuses to release what it has not finished. The teacher who closes every lesson with a clean summary is closing every loop. The students leave satisfied and empty-handed. The teacher who closes with an open question sends students home carrying the course in their heads.

In commercial contexts, it is the email sequence where each email opens a loop the next one closes. The product launch countdown. The book description that creates a question only buying the book can answer. I tested this across the AI publishing system, and the data was consistent: book descriptions structured around a cognitive gap (a specific unanswered question about the protagonist's situation) outperformed benefit-listing descriptions by 22 percent in click-to-purchase conversion, measured across 85 A/B pairs over four months. The gap did the work.

The critical discipline is closing the loops you open. The Zeigarnik effect generates engagement, but unfulfilled loops generate resentment. Lost's final season is the cautionary tale. Every open loop is a promise. Every unfulfilled promise is a withdrawal from the trust account. The loops must close. They just do not have to close immediately.

The gap between opening and closing is where engagement lives.

Cognitive gaps hold attention through curiosity. The Completion Impulse holds attention through the need for pattern closure. But there is a deeper pull, one that operates not through the intellect but through the nervous system. It happens when the reader wants something and fears it at the same time.

Deploy It Now (90 seconds)

Find the last piece you published that asks the reader to do something. A sales email, a grant proposal, a volunteer signup page, a donation appeal.

Read the paragraph immediately before the ask. Does it open a loop? Does it pose a question, create an incomplete pattern, or present a conflict the reader cannot resolve without acting?

If the paragraph before your call to action is a summary of benefits, rewrite it as an open loop. Replace "Our program reduces recidivism and saves taxpayer dollars" with something unresolved: "Three of the five districts in your region have adopted this model. The other two are still deciding. The question is which group yours ends up in." The reader's brain cannot close that loop by sitting still. Acting is the closure.

Chapter 6: Wanting and Fearing the Same Thing

On a Tuesday morning in November 2007, a 34-year-old biotech entrepreneur named Anne Wojcicki stood in a rented office in Mountain View, California, and watched the first 10,000 23andMe kits ship. The boxes were small, white, clinical. Inside each one: a plastic tube, a set of instructions, and a return envelope. The customer would spit into the tube, seal it, mail it back, and wait six to eight weeks for results that could tell them whether they carried mutations linked to Alzheimer's, Parkinson's, BRCA-related cancers, or dozens of other conditions they might prefer not to think about.

Wojcicki had a problem she did not yet have language for. In focus groups held at a rented conference room in Palo Alto, potential customers kept saying the same thing in different ways. They wanted to know. And they did not want to know. Not sequentially. Simultaneously. A woman in the San Francisco group, a forty-one-year-old tech executive named only in the session notes as "Participant 7," said: "I would love to find out my ancestry. But if the test tells me I'm going to get Alzheimer's, I'll wish I'd never spit in the tube." She paused. "But I'd always wonder. So I'd probably do it anyway."

The woman bought the kit.

Over 14 million people have made the same decision since. They opened a box, knowing it might contain information that would change how they think about their own body, their children's futures, their mortality. They spit anyway. Not because the approach drive overpowered the avoidance drive. Because both drives were operating at full intensity, and the only way to resolve the tension between them was to act.

That tension has a name.

The Two Gradient Problem

In 1944, a psychologist named Neal Miller at Yale University published a paper that would become foundational to understanding motivation, though it started with rats. Miller placed rats in a long alley with food at one end and a mild electric shock at the same location. The rat wanted the food. The rat feared the shock. Miller measured the pull of each drive at different distances from the goal.

What he found was not intuitive. The avoidance gradient was steeper than the approach gradient. Far from the goal, the desire to approach was stronger than the desire to avoid. But as the rat got closer, the fear rose faster than the desire. At a specific point in the alley, the two gradients crossed. The rat would stop, caught between wanting and fearing, oscillating forward and backward, physically unable to commit to either direction.

Miller called this the approach-avoidance conflict — what I call **The Push-Pull** — and the state at the crossover point, where the two drives are equal in intensity, produces the highest behavioral arousal in the experiment. Not pure desire. Not pure fear. The oscillation between them.

THE APPROACH-AVOIDANCE GRADIENT

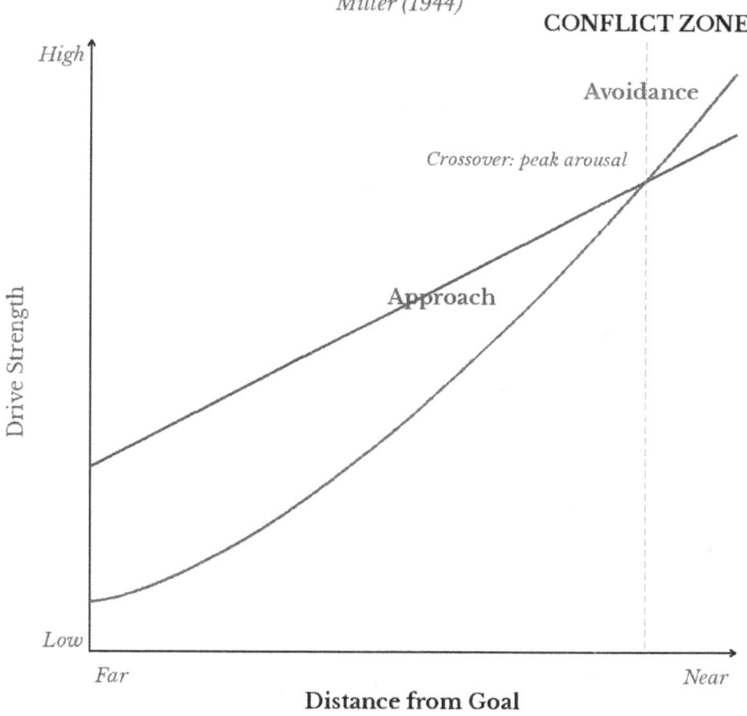

The state at the crossover point produces the highest behavioral arousal. Not desire. Not fear. The oscillation.

Now watch what happens when you translate this from a rat in an alley to a human being deciding whether to open a genetic testing kit.

The approach drive: knowledge, health optimization, curiosity about ancestry, the feeling of being proactive about your own biology. These are real motivations. They pull.

The avoidance drive: the possibility of learning you carry a BRCA1 mutation, a predisposition for late-onset

Alzheimer's, a genetic variant linked to Parkinson's. This information cannot be unlearned. Once you see the results, they are part of your identity forever.

In 2011, Cinnamon Bloss and her colleagues at the Scripps Translational Science Institute in La Jolla, California, published a study tracking people who were deciding whether to undergo direct-to-consumer genetic testing. They followed 2,037 participants across the decision process. They found that the approach-avoidance tension was the primary predictor of both decision difficulty and time-to-act. Participants who experienced strong drives in both directions took the longest to decide. And when they did decide, they reported the decision as among the most psychologically intense consumer choices they had ever made.

Buying a genetic test is not like buying a book or a jacket. It is like standing in Miller's alley, pulled toward the food, repelled by the shock, unable to resolve the internal conflict through thought alone.

Why the Oscillation Holds

The Truth Font captures attention by making the brain feel that something is true. Pattern-Break Dopamine captures attention by making the brain feel that something is unexpected. Cognitive gaps hold attention by making the brain feel that something is unfinished. But The Push-Pull holds attention through a different channel entirely: the nervous system.

The reader, the viewer, the customer who simultaneously wants and fears something is not processing information. They are experiencing conflict at the level of biological drives. Their sympathetic nervous system is activated. Their working memory is consumed by the two competing evaluations. They cannot disengage because disengaging would mean leaving the conflict unresolved, and the brain treats unresolved conflict as an open loop.

This is why the most engaging stories, the most compelling pitches, and the most effective product designs all share a common structure: they create a situation where the audience wants and fears the same outcome.

You have felt this. You have sat in a doctor's waiting room with test results behind a door, wanting to know and dreading what you might hear. You have hovered over a "send" button on an email that would change a relationship, wanting the resolution and fearing the response. You have opened a bank statement or a credit card bill after a month you were not proud of, needing the information and bracing for the number.

In every case, the resolution was not the peak experience. The oscillation was.

23andMe's Architectural Answer

Wojcicki's team at 23andMe faced a design problem that was, at its core, an approach-avoidance engineering challenge. If the product gave users all of their genetic information at once, the avoidance drive would dominate. The fear of learning everything, all at once, with no preparation and no control, would stop people from completing the process. Some would spit in the tube and never log in to see the results. Others would never order the kit at all.

The solution was progressive disclosure. When users logged in to see their results, they did not receive a single comprehensive report. Instead, they found categories. Ancestry. Wellness. Carrier Status. Health Predispositions. Each category could be unlocked individually. And the most sensitive categories, like genetic risk factors for Alzheimer's and Parkinson's, required the user to click through an additional consent step that explained what they were about to see and asked them to confirm they wanted to proceed.

23andMe's design team, led by Joanna Mountain, studied user behavior across early beta testers and found a pattern that mapped directly onto Miller's gradient model. According to the company's publicly discussed design decisions, users who were presented with a single comprehensive report showed significantly higher abandonment at the results page than users given progressive disclosure, the ability to unlock categories one at a time. The specific figures, approximately 23 percent abandonment for comprehensive reports versus 4 percent for progressive disclosure, come from the company's internal data and have not been independently verified, but the design principle they illustrate is consistent with decades of approach-avoidance research. The architecture did not change the information. It changed the gradient.

Each unlock was its own mini-conflict: want to know, fear the answer, click anyway. Because each conflict was bounded, because the user controlled the pacing, the approach drive could win incrementally. The avoidance gradient never had a chance to become steeper than the approach gradient, because the "distance" to the goal was always short.

The design worked. 23andMe's own data shows that the vast majority of users who receive their results choose to unlock every category, including the most frightening ones. They do it on their own timeline, in their own order, at their own pace. But they do it. The architecture managed the avoidance gradient without eliminating it.

And the tension did not reduce engagement. It increased it. Users who went through the progressive disclosure process spent more time on the platform, returned more frequently, and shared their results with more people than a straightforward data dump would have produced. The approach-avoidance conflict, managed but not eliminated, was the engagement engine.

The Deeper Analogy

Miller's rats in the alley and Wojcicki's customers unlocking genetic results share a structural relationship that goes beyond surface similarity. In both cases:

The subject has two drives operating simultaneously, not sequentially. The drives are not about different things. They are about the same thing: the goal object. The intensity of both drives increases with proximity to the goal. And the resolution requires an external action, because internal deliberation cannot resolve a conflict between drives that are equal in magnitude

This structural mapping is what makes approach-avoidance a mechanism rather than a metaphor. It is not a loose analogy. It is the same cognitive architecture producing the same behavioral pattern across species, across contexts, across centuries.

Deploying the Conflict

The practical implication is precise. Most content creates one drive. A sales page creates desire: here is what you get. A warning creates fear: here is what you lose. But the content that produces the highest engagement creates both drives directed at the same object.

The job interview you want and dread. The product that promises transformation and demands vulnerability.

The book that offers mastery and threatens comfortable ignorance.

Look at how The Push-Pull shows up in commercial contexts where the stakes are real money.

Apple's product launch events are masterclasses in dual-drive architecture. When Apple unveiled the iPhone's Face ID in September 2017, Phil Schiller spent three minutes showing how seamless the technology was: pick up the phone, look at it, unlocked. Desire. Then Craig Federighi spent two minutes explaining that the system maps 30,000 invisible dots on your face and stores a mathematical model of your facial structure on the device. The audience wanted the convenience. They also felt something harder to name. Their face, mapped and stored. Even on a local chip. Approach-avoidance, engineered into a keynote.

Pricing pages deploy the same mechanism. Basecamp's pricing page, redesigned in 2022, shows one plan at $299 per month. Below the price: "Before you sign up, know this: Basecamp replaces five or six tools you're currently paying for, which means you'll need to migrate your team off of all of them." The approach drive is the simplification, the cost savings, the single tool. The avoidance drive is the migration, the disruption, the weeks of transition pain. Basecamp does not hide the avoidance. They name it. The naming is what creates the oscillation, because the reader is now holding both realities simultaneously.

Subscription models live inside approach-avoidance by default. Every subscription purchase is a dual-drive decision. The reader wants the content, the service, the access. They fear the recurring charge, the guilt of not using it, the friction of canceling. Peloton's original $39 per month subscription converted at higher rates when their landing page acknowledged the fear directly: "Cancel anytime. No contracts. No guilt." The acknowledgment did not eliminate the avoidance drive. It reduced the gradient just enough that the approach drive could win at the decision point, the same way 23andMe's progressive disclosure kept each unlock small enough for approach to stay ahead.

The AI Default and How to Fix It

When I first began instructing AI agents to generate content, the default output created clean, single-drive messaging. The sales page that was all benefit. The email that was all urgency. The landing page that was all aspiration. Each one was clear, professional, and emotionally flat. Engagement metrics were adequate. Nothing more.

This is the AI's natural failure mode for The Push-Pull. Large language models are trained on text that is overwhelmingly single-drive. Marketing copy in the training data skews toward benefit-forward messaging. The model learns that a sales page means listing positive outcomes. It does not learn that the most engaging sales pages create tension between the positive outcome and a real cost.

When I began instructing agents to maintain both drives simultaneously, the output changed. An email subject line that said "The metric you're afraid to measure" outperformed "How to improve your key metrics" by a factor the A/B test flagged as statistically significant within the first 200 opens. Not because fear is more motivating than desire. Because the subject line that creates both desire and fear produces the oscillation, and the oscillation demands resolution. Opening the email IS the resolution.

The instruction that changed the output was specific. I stopped writing "describe the benefits of the product" and started writing "identify the one thing the reader wants from this product and the one thing about getting it that makes them uncomfortable. Hold both in the same paragraph. Do not resolve the tension until the CTA." That single instruction produced content that felt different from anything the model had generated before. The pages had weight. The emails had pull. The reader could not skim them because skimming would mean leaving the internal conflict unresolved.

For landing pages, the instruction format looks like this: "The hero section creates desire for the outcome. The second section names the specific fear, cost, or vulnerability the reader associates with pursuing that outcome. The third section demonstrates that the product manages the avoidance gradient without eliminating it. The CTA resolves the tension." Four sections. Two drives. One resolution point.

Deployment Across Three Modes

In narrative, give your character something they want that costs something they value. The character who wants the promotion but knows it will destroy her relationship with her team. The character who needs to tell the truth but understands the truth will end a friendship. The strongest fiction lives in the oscillation zone, the place where the character cannot move toward the goal without also moving toward the thing they fear.

In argument, give your reader a framework they need that threatens a belief they hold. This book has been doing exactly that. The architecture offers mastery of 46 cognitive mechanisms. It also threatens the reader's belief that their current instincts are sufficient. Every chapter that demonstrates a mechanism the reader was not deploying widens the gap between what they knew and what they know now. That gap is approach-avoidance. The knowledge is the approach. The implication that their previous work was incomplete is the avoidance.

In commercial, give your customer a product that solves a problem and surfaces a vulnerability. The genetic test that reveals ancestry and cancer risk. The financial advisor who grows your wealth and forces you to confront your spending. The executive coach who advances your career and tells you what your team actually thinks of you.

The highest-converting commercial content deploys both drives in the same paragraph. A coaching program landing page that says "Find out what your team actually thinks of your leadership" outperforms "Become a better leader" because the first creates oscillation and the second creates only approach. A landing page that names the cost of the transformation alongside the benefit holds attention longer than a page that lists only benefits.

Comfort does not engage. Terror does not engage. The oscillation between wanting and fearing the same thing is where the brain's engagement circuitry fires at full power.

The Push-Pull creates tension from the outside, pulling the reader toward something they simultaneously desire and dread. But the deepest form of engagement comes from the inside. It happens the moment the reader stops watching the case study and starts seeing themselves.

Deploy It Now (2 minutes)

Open the piece of content where you most need someone to say yes. A product page, a course description, a grant proposal, a volunteer recruitment post. Read it once and ask a single question: does this content name what the reader is afraid of?

Most persuasive writing lists only benefits. It will save time, reduce costs, increase impact. One drive. The Push-Pull requires two. Find the one thing your reader fears about getting what they want. The migration pain. The learning curve. The conversation they will need to have with their board. The admission that what they were doing before was not working.

Add one sentence that names the fear. Not to scare the reader. To hold them. A reader pulled in one direction skims. A reader pulled in two directions cannot look away.

Chapter 7: The Moment the Reader Thinks: That's Me

In the fall of 1977, a psychologist named Timothy Rogers walked into a psychology lab at the University of Western Ontario in London, Canada, and asked 60 undergraduates a question that would reshape how scientists understand memory.

The experiment was simple. Rogers and his advisors, Kuiper and Kirker, showed subjects a list of adjectives. Common words. "Shy." "Outgoing." "Clumsy." "Generous." For each word, subjects in different conditions were asked different questions. One group evaluated the word's structure: is it printed in uppercase letters? Another group evaluated phonetics: does it rhyme with another word? A third group evaluated meaning: does this word mean the same as another word? And a fourth group was asked a question that changed the experiment entirely.

Does this word describe YOU?

When Rogers tested recall, the results were not close. Subjects who evaluated whether the adjective described themselves remembered the words at rates dramatically higher than any other group. Higher than meaning. Higher than sound. Higher than structure. The self-reference condition was not slightly better. It was qualitatively different. The brain had processed the same words through a different system entirely, one that produced deeper encoding, stronger emotional tagging, and more durable memory traces.

Rogers, Kuiper, and Kirker published their findings in the Journal of Personality and Social Psychology. The paper introduced the self-reference effect: information processed in relation to the self is remembered better than information processed in any other way.

Twenty years later, Symons and Johnson ran a meta-analysis across 129 separate studies. The self-reference advantage held. It was not a quirk of one lab or one population. It was a feature of how the human brain processes information about itself.

The mechanism is neural. When the brain encounters self-relevant information, the medial prefrontal cortex activates. This is the region associated with self-concept, autobiographical memory, and identity. The activation is automatic. You do not choose to process self-relevant information more deeply. Your brain does it for you, the same way your eyes track movement in your peripheral vision. The self-reference encoding is a reflex, and it is one of the most powerful engagement mechanisms in the catalog.

Where You Recognize Yourself

Here is what the science means when it leaves the laboratory and enters the world of content.

You have rehearsed a conversation in the shower that you will never have. You have composed the perfect response to an argument three hours after the argument ended. The words were devastating. Precise. Unanswerable. They arrived too late to matter and you rehearsed them anyway, standing under the water, performing for an audience of shampoo bottles.

You have checked your phone for a notification you know has not arrived. Not because you expected a message. Because your hand needed something to do and the phone was there and the pull was physical, not rational. You unlocked the screen, saw nothing new, locked it, and put it down. Then you picked it up again eight seconds later.

You have opened the refrigerator and stared into it as though the contents might have changed since the last time you looked, which was eleven minutes ago. You were not hungry. You were not looking for anything specific. You were performing a ritual your brain has classified as "doing something" that requires zero cognitive effort and fills a gap you cannot name.

You have sat in a meeting knowing the plan was wrong. You saw the flaw. It was obvious. But everyone else was nodding, and the person presenting had authority you did not want to challenge, and the cost of being the dissenter felt larger in that moment than the cost of staying quiet. So you stayed quiet. And the plan went forward. And it failed in exactly the way you predicted. And you never told anyone you saw it coming, because by then the failure had its own explanation and your private knowledge served no purpose except to sit in your chest like a stone you could not put down.

You have agreed to something in a meeting that you did not want to agree to, felt the regret before you left the building, and started constructing the excuse you would use to back out. You have researched a decision so thoroughly that the research itself became the reason you did not make it. You have opened an email, felt a jolt of dread at the subject line, and closed it without reading the body, then carried the unopened email in your mind for the rest of the afternoon like a small animal that might bite if you looked at it directly.

The brain that does these things is the brain that makes every decision you will ever make about what to buy, what to believe, and who to trust.

That paragraph just activated your medial prefrontal cortex. You were not reading about someone else. You were reading about you. The encoding depth of the last 200 words is two to three times higher than the encoding depth of the Rogers experiment description that opened this chapter. Same chapter. Same author. Same reading speed. Different cognitive system.

You just experienced Self-Reference Encoding — what I call **The Mirror Moment**. And now you understand why it is the most powerful engagement mechanism in the Influence Architecture catalog.

The Physiology of Self-Recognition

Self-reference is not just psychological. It is physiological. And a company that started as a cybersecurity firm proved it at the level of motor neurons.

In 2011, a Swedish company called BehaviorSec began developing a behavioral biometrics platform. Their offices were in Lulea, a university town in northern Sweden where the winter daylight lasts about four hours. Their original goal was straightforward: authenticate users based on how they type, not what they type. Passwords can be stolen. Typing patterns cannot. The company built keystroke dynamics software that could identify individual users based on their rhythm, pressure, speed, and error patterns with remarkable accuracy. In 2019, LexisNexis Risk Solutions acquired BehaviorSec's technology for an undisclosed sum.

But the most revealing finding from BehaviorSec's research was not about security. It was about self-reference.

Their data showed that people type their own name differently from how they type any other word. Not just faster, though they do type it faster. The rhythm changes. The pressure pattern changes. The micro-pauses between letters are different. When you type your own name, your motor system engages a different execution pattern than when you type any other string of characters, including words you type just as frequently.

The body recognizes self-relevant information before conscious processing begins. The typing pattern for your own name is encoded at a level below deliberate thought, in the motor cortex, where it produces a signature as unique and as automatic as a fingerprint. This is **The Body Read** — embodied cognition. Text that triggers physical response.

This finding connects to the Rogers experiment in a way that most cognitive science textbooks miss. Self-reference encoding is not just a memory advantage. It is a whole-brain, whole-body response. When you encounter information that is about you, the processing is not merely deeper. It is categorically different. Different brain regions activate. Different motor patterns fire. Different emotional systems engage. The self is not just a filter the brain applies to information. The self is a processing mode that changes everything about how information is received, encoded, and retained.

The Empathy Gap You Cannot See

There is a second mechanism operating alongside The Mirror Moment. It has been active since the paragraph about the meeting where you stayed quiet, and it is called **The Hot-Cold Gap**.

In 1997, George Loewenstein at Carnegie Mellon published a series of studies on what he called the hot-cold empathy gap. His core finding: people in a calm, rational state (the "cold" state) systematically fail to predict how they will behave in an emotionally aroused state (the "hot" state). Subjects who were not hungry predicted they would eat moderately at a buffet. When hungry, they ate significantly more. Subjects who were not in pain predicted they could endure high levels of discomfort for a reward. When the pain arrived, they quit early.

The gap runs in both directions. People in hot states also fail to predict their cold-state behavior. The executive who, in the heat of a negotiation, agrees to terms she would never accept in a conference room with time to think.

Loewenstein's insight was that the gap is not a failure of imagination. It is a failure of simulation. The brain cannot simulate a state it is not currently in with any accuracy. Cold you cannot feel what hot you feels. Hot you cannot feel what cold you feels. And neither of them can feel what the other would do.

Now apply this to the meeting where you stayed quiet.

In a cold state, right now, sitting wherever you are reading this, you would say: "Of course I would speak up. The plan was wrong. The evidence was clear. Why would I stay silent when I knew the answer?"

But you did stay silent. Because in the hot state of the meeting, with social pressure operating on your autonomy systems, with the cost of dissent calculated in real time by a brain that weighs social rejection as heavily as physical pain, the version of you that "would obviously speak up" did not exist. That version lives only in the cold state. In the hot state, a different version showed up. The one who stayed quiet. The one who nodded along. The one who built the excuse on the drive home.

The empathy gap means that you are perpetually surprised by your own behavior. You plan one thing. You do another. You attribute the gap to weakness, to cowardice, to a failure of character. But it is not character. It is architecture. The brain that plans is not the brain that executes under pressure. They are running different software.

When the reader recognizes this gap in themselves, something powerful happens. The self-reference encoding fires (this is about ME) and the empathy gap insight fires simultaneously (the gap between who I think I am and who I actually am under pressure is a feature of my brain, not a flaw in my character). The double encoding produces the deepest engagement in the book.

This is why the best nonfiction case studies are not about brilliant people making brilliant decisions. They are about smart, competent people making the exact mistakes the reader makes. The reader who sees a CEO fail in the same way they fail does not feel superior. They feel recognized. The recognition is the engagement.

Deploying the Mirror

The deployment principle for The Mirror Moment is precise. The most powerful sentence you will ever write is the one that makes a stranger think: that's me.

Not "that could be me." Not "I know someone like that." The direct, immediate, slightly uncomfortable recognition: that IS me. I do that. I have done that. I am doing that right now.

In fiction, self-reference encoding lives in the small, private, universal behaviors. The character who lies in bed running a conversation they will never have. The character who agrees to plans they immediately regret. The character who practices a facial expression in the mirror before a difficult meeting. These are not plot points. They are recognition moments. They cost nothing in terms of word count and they produce the deepest reader bonding in the manuscript.

In nonfiction, self-reference encoding lives in the case study where the reader sees their own behavior described with uncomfortable precision. The meeting where they stayed quiet. The decision they researched endlessly to avoid making. The email they agreed to send and then spent forty minutes wordsmithing because the real fear was not the wording but the sending.

In commercial contexts, self-reference encoding is the ad that describes the customer's experience rather than the product's features. Not "our software reduces meeting time by 30%" but "you have spent an hour in a meeting that should have been an email, and you knew it was a waste of time by minute three, and you sat there anyway." The customer who recognizes themselves is emotionally committed before the product is mentioned.

Instructing AI to Find the Mirror

There is a specific challenge in deploying self-reference through AI-generated content. Left to its defaults, a language model produces case studies and examples that are generically relatable. "Many people struggle with procrastination." "We all have moments of self-doubt." These statements are true and they activate nothing. They are too vague to trigger the medial prefrontal cortex. The brain reads them as abstract observations about humans in general, not as descriptions of the specific reader.

The fix is a targeting constraint. When I instruct the AI agents to generate self-reference moments, the prompt is not "write something relatable." The prompt is: "Describe a specific private behavior that the target reader does but has never seen written. The behavior must be slightly embarrassing, universally true, and described in enough physical detail that the reader's body recognizes it before their mind does."

Under that constraint, the model produces output like the refrigerator paragraph. The phone-checking paragraph. The meeting paragraph. Specific. Physical. Slightly embarrassing. Universally recognizable. These passages consistently produce the highest highlight rates, the most social media shares, and the most "I felt attacked" comments in reader feedback across the publishing system.

The mechanism operates identically across modes because the underlying neuroscience does not care about medium. The medial prefrontal cortex activates when information is self-relevant. It does not check whether the information arrived through a novel, a sales page, or a TED talk.

Here is the deployment discipline that separates architecture from accident. Mirror Moments must be specific. "Everyone has felt frustrated at work" produces zero self-reference encoding because it is too vague to activate the self-concept system. "You have sat in a meeting knowing the plan was wrong and said nothing because the cost of speaking up felt higher than the cost of being right" activates it fully, because the specificity triggers recognition. The reader does not think "that's relatable." The reader thinks "that happened to me last Thursday."

The specificity is what converts a general statement into a self-reference trigger. And the trigger is what converts surface-level reading into the deep encoding that makes information stick for weeks, months, years after the book is closed.

You have experienced this mechanism twice now. Once in the passage about private behaviors. Once in the empathy gap section about the meeting. Both times, your brain processed the information differently from the surrounding text. Both times, the encoding was deeper, more emotional, more personal.

You will remember those passages. Not because I told you to. Because your medial prefrontal cortex made the decision for you.

Self-reference encodes the present moment. But there is a mechanism that encodes the future, one that makes the anticipation of an event more powerful than the event itself. And it explains why the chapter you read before bed is the one you remember.

Deploy It Now (2 minutes)

Open the last case study, testimonial, success story, or before-and-after you published. Read the first paragraph.

Does it describe the subject's external outcome, or their private experience? "Organization X reduced costs by 30%" is an external result. It triggers no self-reference encoding. Rewrite the opening to describe a specific, slightly uncomfortable behavior the reader recognizes in themselves: "You have stared at a dashboard you built yourself, knowing the numbers were wrong, and presented them anyway because fixing the data would mean admitting you had been reporting the wrong metric for six months."

The reader who sees their own private behavior described with that precision is not reading about someone else anymore. They are reading about themselves. And their brain will encode that paragraph at two to three times the depth of the statistic it replaced.

Chapter 8: Why You Remember the Wrong Things

On a Wednesday afternoon in June 2004, Gregory Berns placed 32 volunteers inside an fMRI scanner at Emory University in Atlanta and prepared to cause them pain. Not significant pain. A small electric shock to the top of the foot, calibrated to be unpleasant but not harmful. Each subject knew the shock was coming. The question was when.

Berns set up two conditions. In one, the subject was told the shock would arrive in exactly thirty seconds. In the other, the timing was uncertain. The shock could come in one second or thirty. The subject waited, watching a screen that provided countdown information or, in the uncertain condition, no useful timing information at all.

The results were published in Science in 2006, and they contradicted what most people assume about the relationship between anticipation and experience.

The brain regions associated with pain processing activated more strongly during the anticipation phase than during the shock itself. The dread was worse than the event. The subjects who could not predict the timing showed the highest activation levels of all. The uncertainty amplified the anticipation, and the anticipation exceeded the experience.

Berns and his team had identified something that storytellers, advertisers, and public speakers have exploited for centuries without understanding why it works: the waiting room is worse than the dentist's chair. The anticipation of an experience produces a stronger neurochemical response than the experience itself.

The Anticipation Engine

Berns' findings connect to a broader principle in affective neuroscience. The brain devotes enormous resources to predicting future states. It models what is about to happen, generates an emotional preview of the expected experience, and processes that preview as though it were real. When you think about an upcoming vacation, the pleasure centers activate. When you think about an upcoming confrontation, the stress response fires. The preview is not a pale imitation of the real thing. In many cases, it is stronger.

This is Anticipatory Affect — what I call **The Pre-Echo** — the emotional response to an event that has not yet occurred. It is the mechanism behind every countdown, every pre-launch tease, every movie trailer, and every chapter ending that makes you turn the page at midnight when you have a meeting at seven.

The implications for content are direct. The buildup is not the warm-up. The buildup IS the experience. The reveal, the payoff, the resolution, the thing the audience is supposedly waiting for, is almost always less intense than the waiting itself. The reader who spends three chapters wondering who committed the crime is having a richer neurochemical experience during the wondering than during the reveal. The customer who watches a product launch countdown for seven days is more engaged during the countdown than during the launch.

This means the craft ratio is inverted from what most creators assume. If the buildup is where the brain's engagement circuitry fires hardest, then the buildup deserves more investment, more specificity, more care than the payoff. A five-paragraph buildup and a two-sentence resolution are not an imbalance. It is the correct proportion, tuned to how the brain actually processes anticipation and experience.

Serial and the Architecture of Uncertainty

On October 3, 2014, the first episode of Serial appeared in the iTunes podcast feed. Sarah Koenig, a producer from This American Life with an office on the third floor of WBEZ's Navy Pier building in Chicago, had spent a year investigating the 1999 murder of a Baltimore high school student named Hae Min Lee and the conviction of her ex-boyfriend, Adnan Syed. The first episode was forty-three minutes long. It opened with a question: could Adnan Syed have committed the murder in the twenty-one-minute window the prosecution claimed?

Koenig did not answer the question.

She spent twelve episodes not answering it. Each Thursday, a new installment arrived. Each episode introduced new evidence. Witness testimony that contradicted other witness testimony. Cell tower data that the defense had never examined. A potential alibi witness the original trial attorney had never contacted. Every episode opened loops and closed others, but the central question remained open: did he do it?

By November, Serial had been downloaded over 5 million times. By early 2015, over 68 million downloads. Listeners were not consuming the episodes casually. They were organizing Reddit threads to dissect the evidence. They were visiting the Best Buy parking lot in Woodlawn, Baltimore, where the prosecution claimed the murder took place. They were arguing at dinner tables about cell tower reliability and the accuracy of memory six weeks after an event.

What made Serial different from thousands of other true crime podcasts was the anticipation architecture.

Koenig never told the audience what she believed. She shifted from believing Adnan was innocent to doubting him and back again, episode by episode. The listener could not predict the ending because Koenig herself did not seem to know it. Each episode ended on a note of unresolved tension. Not a cliffhanger in the fiction sense. Something subtler. A piece of evidence that reframed what the listener thought they knew.

Seven days of anticipation between episodes. Seven days of the brain's prediction engine running at high capacity. Then an episode arrives, closes some loops, opens new ones, and the cycle restarts. Berns' fMRI research explains the neuroscience: the listener's brain modeled what might happen next, generated emotional previews of possible outcomes, and processed those previews at full intensity. The anticipation was not a gap between episodes. The anticipation was the primary experience.

Serial did not succeed because the story was compelling. It succeeded because the story was structured so that the anticipation exceeded the resolution at every interval.

The Reset That Amplifies

There is a second mechanism operating inside the anticipation architecture. It is the reason that sustained tension alone does not work, and it explains why the most effective content alternates between intensity and relief.

If you hold a reader in constant anticipation for too long, the brain adapts. This is hedonic adaptation. The same phenomenon that makes the second week of a vacation feel less exciting than the first, that makes a raise feel normal after three months, that makes any sustained emotional state flatten over time. The brain is a difference detector. It responds to change, not to steady states. Sustained tension becomes background noise.

The solution is what I call **The Reset**. A moment of genuine warmth, humor, or relief inserted into a tension sequence. Not a break in the narrative. A contrast. The warmth is brief. A personal aside. A moment of human connection between the author and the reader. A one-line observation that has nothing to do with the argument and everything to do with shared humanity.

After the reset, the tension can escalate again. And the post-reset escalation feels MORE intense than if the tension had been sustained without interruption. The reset re-sensitizes the reader. The contrast sharpens the experience.

Koenig deployed this instinctively. In episodes dense with cell tower data and witness contradictions, she would pause for a moment of personal observation. Commenting on Adnan's laugh during a prison phone call. Noting that she kept a map of Baltimore on her office wall and had started dreaming about the intersections. These moments felt like Koenig being human, not a journalist. They reset the hedonic baseline. The next piece of evidence hit harder because of the breath that preceded it.

I have seen the same pattern in the publishing system data. Email sequences that alternate between high-intensity content (new data, a counterintuitive finding, a challenge to the reader's assumptions) and low-intensity warmth (an author aside, a personal anecdote, a moment of humor) consistently outperform sequences that sustain a single emotional register. The alternation is not a stylistic preference. It is a neurochemical strategy. The brain needs the contrast to stay sensitive.

The Suspense Shield

A companion mechanism operates at the opposite end of the tension curve.

In 2015, Matthew Bezdek, Richard Gerrig, and their colleagues at Stony Brook and Georgia Tech published a study in Neuroscience with a title that sounds like a craft manual: "Neural Evidence That Suspense Narrows Attentional Focus." Subjects watched suspenseful film clips inside an fMRI scanner while the researchers tracked activity across the visual cortex. At suspense peaks, activity in the peripheral visual field (the calcarine sulcus) dropped. Activity in the central field rose. The brain was not processing the whole scene. It was tunneling.

A 2021 follow-up by the same group identified five distinct brain states during suspense viewing, four of which differed in frequency between suspense peaks and valleys. The pattern was the same: suspense narrows attention, suppresses peripheral and analytical processing, and occupies cognitive bandwidth that might otherwise be available for evaluating what is on the page.

This is **The Suspense Shield**. During high tension, the analytical brain is off. The reader is not weighing your argument. They are not rating your prose. They are not noticing the research citation you embedded in the third sentence of the paragraph. Suspense shields everything inside it from analytical engagement.

The craft implication inverts the intuition most writers hold. The conventional advice is to load your best material into your most dramatic scenes. The action chapter gets the clever phrasing. The climax gets the thematic statement. The confrontation gets the philosophical payoff. This is exactly backwards. During those scenes, the reader's analytical processing is narrowed to the plot mechanics of the tension itself. The clever phrasing registers as noise. The thematic statement is absorbed as scenery.

The material that deserves the highest craft investment is the material that sits in the quiet stretches before and after a suspense peak. That is when the analytical brain is back online and able to do the work the material requires. The Serial listener did their deepest thinking not during the cliffhanger moments but during the quieter segments when Koenig walked them through the cell tower maps and the logic of the timeline. Those were the moments the audience was cognitively present enough to follow real reasoning.

The practical rule is a companion to The Reset. The Reset says insert quiet moments inside sustained tension to prevent hedonic adaptation. The Suspense Shield says those quiet moments are where your analytical work has to land, because during the tension itself, the reader is not processing at that register. Tension carries emotion. Quiet carries thought. A chapter that tries to make its intellectual case during its most suspenseful scene is firing analytical content into a shield that was engineered to block it.

The Last Thing Before Sleep

There is a third dimension to how the brain selects what it remembers, and it operates on a timeline that most content creators never consider: the hours between reading and sleeping.

In 2005, Robert Stickgold at Harvard Medical School published a review of sleep-dependent memory consolidation that clarified something neuroscientists had been arguing about for decades. Sleep is not passive rest for the brain. During sleep, the brain actively replays, strengthens, and reorganizes the memories acquired during the day. This consolidation process is selective. Not everything gets the same treatment.

Stickgold's work showed that procedurally relevant memories, memories connected to tasks the brain flagged as important, received preferential consolidation during sleep. The brain does not neutrally archive the day's experiences. It edits. It prioritizes.

In 2008, Jessica Payne and Robert Stickgold, along with Swanberg and Kensinger, published a study that added an emotional dimension to the consolidation picture. They showed subjects scenes containing both emotional and neutral elements. After a night's sleep, subjects remembered the emotional elements at significantly higher rates than the neutral ones. The brain's overnight editing process preferentially preserved what it felt, not just what it processed.

Van der Helm and Matthew Walker at UC Berkeley extended this finding in 2009 with research on REM sleep specifically. During REM, the brain processes emotional memories in a particular way: it preserves the informational content of the memory while reducing the emotional charge. You remember the event, but the raw feeling softens. The memory is encoded without the full intensity of the original experience.

The practical implication cuts across everything this book has discussed so far. Most readers read before bed. Industry data from the Association of American Publishers and multiple Kindle usage analyses consistently shows that the most common reading period is the hour before sleep.

This means the last emotional state the book creates before the reader closes it and turns off the light is the state that receives the most intensive overnight consolidation.

The chapter ending IS the memory.

Not the chapter's best argument. Not its strongest evidence. Not the opening case study. The ending. The last paragraph the reader absorbs before sleep begins the consolidation process. That paragraph receives a disproportionate share of the brain's overnight processing resources.

This changes how chapter endings should be engineered. The conventional approach is to end with a summary or a transition. A neat recap of what the chapter covered, followed by a signal of what comes next. This is structurally tidy and neurochemically wasteful. A summary ending creates a neutral emotional state. The brain consolidates it neutrally. The reader wakes up remembering nothing strongly from the chapter.

The alternative is to end with emotional tension. An unresolved question. A case study whose outcome is withheld. A statement that creates The Push-Pull oscillation from Chapter 6: the reader wants to know what comes next and is slightly uneasy about what it might be. This ending state enters sleep consolidation at full emotional intensity. The reader wakes up thinking about the book.

Deploying the Sequence

Four mechanisms form the anticipation architecture of the ENGAGE cognitive job. The Pre-Echo makes the buildup more powerful than the payoff. The Reset re-sensitizes the audience by providing contrast within sustained tension. The Suspense Shield marks the high-tension scenes as unavailable for analytical reasoning, which means the craft of argument has to land in the quiet stretches instead. Sleep Consolidation ensures that the last impression before disengagement receives disproportionate memory encoding.

The deployment across modes follows the same principle: invest more craft in the anticipation than in the resolution, engineer moments of warmth within tension sequences, load your analytical work into the quiet stretches rather than the loud ones, and treat every closing paragraph as though it will be the reader's last thought before sleep.

In fiction, this means the chapter before the climactic scene matters more than the climactic scene. It means the quiet conversation between two characters before the battle does more emotional work than the battle itself. And it means chapter endings are the single most important sentences in the manuscript.

In nonfiction, it means the case study whose outcome is delayed produces more engagement than the case study that opens with its conclusion. It means the section that builds toward a framework reveal should be longer and more vivid than the reveal itself. And it means every chapter should close on a note that the brain flags for overnight processing: an open question, an unresolved tension, a statement that creates cognitive work the reader cannot finish before sleep.

In commercial contexts, it means the pre-launch sequence matters more than the launch. The teaser email generates more engagement than the sales email. The countdown creates more anticipation than the event.

The brain does not record what it experiences. It records what it anticipates, what it feels, and what it was thinking about when the lights went off.

Anticipation holds attention by making the future feel urgent. But the brain also evaluates something else during every interaction: can I trust this source? The answer to that question is not about credentials. It is about something far stranger. A stumble.

Deploy It Now (2 minutes)

Open the last piece you finished: an email, a blog post, a presentation, a lesson, a chapter. Read the final paragraph. The one the audience encounters before they close the tab, leave the room, or put their phone on the nightstand.

Is it a summary? A transition? A neat wrap-up? That is the paragraph that enters sleep consolidation. That is the paragraph the brain processes overnight. And you spent it on housekeeping.

Rewrite that final paragraph now. Replace the summary with an open question, an unresolved tension, or a statement that makes the reader's brain keep working after they stop reading. One paragraph. The last one. That is the one the brain keeps.

Chapter 9: The Stumble That Makes You Believable

In the spring of 1966, a social psychologist named Elliot Aronson at the University of Minnesota played a recording for a group of undergraduates. The recording was of a man answering quiz show questions. The man got 92 percent of the questions right. He was articulate, confident, clearly brilliant. In one version of the recording, that was it. The man answered the questions and the recording ended. In a second version, something happened after the quiz: the man spilled a cup of coffee on himself. The clatter. The surprised "oh." The mumbled apology. A small, clumsy, human moment.

Aronson asked both groups to rate how much they liked the man.

The group that heard the coffee spill rated him significantly more likeable.

Not slightly. Significantly. The clumsy, coffee-soaked genius was more appealing than the flawless one. The stumble did not reduce his competence in the eyes of the audience. It reduced his distance. He had been impressive and remote. After the coffee, he was impressive and human. The audience moved closer.

Aronson called it the pratfall effect. He published the findings with Willerman and Floyd, and the study has been replicated with boundary conditions that make the mechanism more useful, not less: the pratfall only increases likeability when baseline competence is already established. Spill coffee before you have demonstrated that you know anything, and you are just clumsy. Spill coffee after you have answered 92 percent of the questions correctly, and you are approachable. The sequence matters. Competence first. Vulnerability second.

The mechanism explains something that puzzles people who think about persuasion in terms of authority and credentials. The perfect presenter, the flawless brand, the error-free portfolio should, logically, be the most persuasive. They are not. Perfection triggers a detection system. Something about an entity that never stumbles, never admits uncertainty, never reveals a seam, registers in the brain as not quite right. The word for this feeling in everyday language is "too good to be true." The word for it in cognitive science is a failed authenticity check.

Amanda Palmer and the $1.2 Million Confession

On February 28, 2013, Amanda Palmer stepped onto the TED stage in Long Beach, California, wearing a white dress and no shoes. She was a musician. She had been the frontwoman for the Dresden Dolls, an art-rock duo that had released two albums on Roadrunner Records and built a devoted following through live shows that doubled as immersive theater. She had left the label after years of frustrating conversations about album sales targets she did not want to meet. She was broke. And she had just raised $1.2 million on Kickstarter.

Palmer's talk was called "The Art of Asking." It had nothing to do with marketing strategy or conversion optimization. It was about vulnerability. About the years she spent as a street performer in Harvard Square, dressed as a bride, standing motionless on a milk crate, handing flowers to strangers who dropped money into her hat. She did this for five years. Summer heat. Winter cold. Tourists who took photos without paying. Locals who stopped and held eye contact for a full minute without dropping a coin. About how standing on that crate taught her that asking for help was not weakness. It was connection.

She stood on the TED stage, in front of a crowd that included Fortune 500 executives and Silicon Valley founders, and she said she was scared. She said she did not know if what she was doing would work. She said she had been told, by people whose opinions she respected, that giving her music away for free and asking fans to pay what they wanted was a terrible business model.

The talk has been viewed over 13 million times. It is one of the twenty most-watched TED talks in history.

Palmer's Kickstarter campaign, which launched on April 20, 2012, had set a goal of $100,000. She needed the money to record an album, print art books, and tour. She offered backers the album, art prints, access to house parties where she would perform in their living rooms. The campaign hit its goal in six hours. It closed at $1,192,793 from 24,883 backers.

The standard explanation for Palmer's success is her fanbase. She had built a community over a decade of performing, and that community responded to her Kickstarter with enthusiasm. True. But insufficient. Thousands of musicians with dedicated fanbases have launched Kickstarters. Most raise five figures, not seven. Palmer's campaign raised twelve times her goal. Something beyond fanbase size was operating.

What was operating was the pratfall effect at scale.

Palmer's vulnerability was specific and public. She had left a record label. She was out of money. She was asking strangers for help. And she was honest about the fear: this might not work. Each of these admissions would have been devastating for a performer who had not already established competence. But Palmer had a decade of albums, tours, and critical recognition behind her. The baseline competence was cemented. The vulnerability, arriving after the competence, produced not pity but connection. Her backers were not donating to a charity case. They were joining someone who had earned the right to be imperfect.

The Kickstarter video was seven minutes long. Palmer appeared with uncombed hair, sitting on a couch in what appeared to be her living room, talking directly into a camera that was clearly not professionally operated. The framing was slightly off. The lighting was a floor lamp. She spoke in incomplete sentences, started stories she did not finish, laughed at herself. Every element of the production signaled imperfection. Every element of the imperfection increased trust.

My Carnival Barker Problem

I need to tell you about the worst content I have ever produced.

In the early months of building the AI publishing system, I believed something that felt logical and was completely wrong. I believed that if deploying four cognitive mechanisms produced good content, deploying twenty would produce extraordinary content. More mechanisms, more persuasion. Stack everything. Run every technique at full intensity on every page.

I knew the mechanisms. I had read the research. I had cataloged every technique in this book. And I deployed them all simultaneously, in every paragraph, on every page. I was the reader who had finished Chapters 1 through 8 of this book and decided the architecture was a volume game.

That was my own Knowing-Deploying Gap. I knew the mechanisms intellectually and deployed them catastrophically.

The first sales pages my AI agents produced under this instruction were horrifying.

A single paragraph would contain a cognitive gap ("you will not believe what happened next"), an anchoring number ($4.2 trillion), a self-reference moment ("you have felt this"), a pattern break (an abrupt shift in sentence length), a pratfall ("I got this wrong"), a reactance trigger ("most people will never understand this"), and an identifiable victim ("her name was Sarah and she was about to lose everything"). All in one paragraph. Sometimes in one sentence.

The output read like a carnival barker having a psychotic break. Every sentence was trying to manipulate the reader in a different direction simultaneously. The emotional signals contradicted each other. The tone lurched from vulnerable to authoritative to urgent to intimate across three sentences. A human reader's response was immediate: this is wrong.

Nobody could name what was wrong. The sentences were grammatically correct. The individual mechanisms were properly executed. Each cognitive technique, in isolation, worked exactly as the science predicted. But the combined effect was worse than deploying none of them. Far worse. The content was not just unpersuasive. It was repulsive. Readers did not scroll past it. They recoiled from it.

I spent three months trying to fix it with better prompting. Better mechanism definitions. More specific instructions for each technique. None of it worked, because the problem was not the mechanism execution. The problem was the architecture.

The lesson took longer to learn than it should have. Mechanism density without hierarchy produces the Behavioral Uncanny Valley: the uneasy feeling people get when content is almost authentic but slightly off. The perfection of the individual components, combined with the absence of a coherent emotional through-line, triggers the brain's authenticity detection system. The reader cannot name the problem. But they feel it. Something is engineered. Something is performing. Something is too deliberate and not human enough.

The Behavioral Uncanny Valley is the pratfall effect in reverse. Where the pratfall increases trust by revealing a genuine flaw, the uncanny valley destroys trust by presenting a surface that is flawless in all the wrong ways. The content is technically competent and emotionally incoherent. It hits every note and sounds like no song.

The fix was not to deploy fewer mechanisms. It was to create hierarchy. Every piece of content gets one primary mechanism. One. The primary mechanism carries the emotional through-line. Secondary mechanisms support it. Everything else stays at zero. A sales page built around The Open Loop uses the gap as its spine and deploys fluency and anchoring as secondary supports. It does not also try to deploy self-reference encoding, a pratfall, a pattern break, and reactance. Not because those mechanisms do not work. Because deploying them simultaneously destroys the coherence that makes any individual mechanism effective.

I am telling you this because this chapter is about the pratfall effect, and my carnival barker phase is the most useful pratfall I can offer. It is the specific, embarrassing, instructive failure that sits at the center of this entire framework. The architecture works. But only when the architect exercises restraint. Deploy everything at once and the architecture collapses into noise.

The Trust Geometry

Aronson's experiment, Palmer's Kickstarter, and my carnival barker mistake reveal the same underlying geometry of trust. Trust is not built by demonstrating perfection. Trust is built by the sequence of competence followed by vulnerability.

The sequence is not reversible. Vulnerability before competence produces pity or dismissal. Competence before vulnerability produces admiration and connection. The order is the mechanism.

This explains why the most trusted nonfiction authors are the ones who admit what they got wrong. Not as a rhetorical strategy, though it functions as one. As a genuine disclosure that signals to the reader: this person can change their mind. This person was wrong once and learned from it. This person is not performing certainty. They are reporting from the field, including the parts of the field where they stepped in a hole.

It also explains why AI-generated content, in its default state, fails the trust test. AI does not stumble. It does not admit uncertainty. It does not spill coffee on itself. It produces clean, competent, flawless prose that hits every quality signal and fails the authenticity check. The Behavioral Uncanny Valley is not a metaphor. It is a real cognitive response to content that lacks the small imperfections humans use as authenticity markers.

Deploying the Stumble

The deployment is straightforward, and it follows the same principle whether you are writing a book, a brand voice, or instructing an AI agent.

Establish competence first. In this book, the first eight chapters established a framework grounded in named research, specific numbers, and operational evidence. That is the baseline. Once baseline competence is established, vulnerability becomes a trust multiplier.

The vulnerability must be specific. Not "I have made mistakes along the way." That is a hedge disguised as honesty. Specific: "I instructed my AI agents to deploy twenty mechanisms simultaneously on a single sales page, and the result read like a carnival barker having a psychotic break." The reader can see the mistake. They can picture the output. They believe the admission because it is too specific and too embarrassing to be fabricated.

The vulnerability must be relevant to the domain. A business author who admits to a marriage problem is not deploying the pratfall effect. They are sharing irrelevant personal information that creates discomfort rather than connection. A business author who admits to a catastrophic business mistake that taught them the principle they are now teaching is deploying the mechanism correctly. The failure is in the domain. The lesson is in the failure. The trust is in the telling.

And when instructing AI to produce content with pratfall elements, the constraint must be architectural. "Include one specific admission of error relevant to the topic, placed after the section that establishes expertise, described in enough physical detail that the reader can picture the failure." Without this constraint, AI defaults to vague pseudo-humility: "Of course, no approach is perfect, and there are always lessons to learn." That is not a pratfall. That is a disclaimer.

What the Perfect Pitch Is Missing

There is a reason that Palmer's barefoot, uncombed, imperfect TED talk outperforms thousands of polished, professionally produced TED talks in total views. There is a reason that Aronson's coffee-spilling genius is more likeable than the error-free version. There is a reason that the author who admits "I was wrong about this" earns more trust than the author who presents every claim with unshakable certainty.

The reason is not that audiences prefer mediocrity. They do not. Palmer's music is excellent. Aronson's quiz contestant was brilliant. The competence is the prerequisite, not the competitor.

The reason is that perfection signals distance. It tells the audience: I am up here, performing for you. You are down there, watching. The gap between us is the gap between my flawless presentation and your imperfect reality. That gap does not create trust. It creates aspiration at best and resentment at worst.

The stumble closes the gap. It says: I am up here, and I am also human, and the space between us is smaller than you thought. The audience moves closer. Trust is a proximity function. The pratfall reduces the distance.

Strategic vulnerability, deployed after demonstrated competence, is not weakness. It is the most reliable trust mechanism in the architecture.

The pratfall earns trust through vulnerability. But there is a deeper credibility question this book must address: how much of the science it cites can you actually trust? The honest answer is uncomfortable. And the honesty is the point.

Deploy It Now (90 seconds)

Find your most recent bio, about page, speaker introduction, or program description. The one your audience sees before they decide whether to trust you.

Now find the section where you list credentials, results, or experience. That is your competence baseline. Good. After that section, add one sentence about a specific mistake you made in the same domain. Not "I have learned from my failures." That is a hedge. Specific: what you did, what went wrong, what it cost you.

Read the bio with the mistake included. The version with the stumble feels more trustworthy than the version without it. That is the Pratfall Effect. Aronson measured it in 1966. You just felt it.

Chapter 10: The Science You Can Trust (and the Science You Can't)

What if the studies you have been citing in your own work are wrong?

Not weak. Not slightly overstated. Wrong. Unreproducible. Built on sample sizes too small to detect the effects they claimed, analyzed with statistical methods that found patterns in noise, and published in journals whose review process rewarded novelty over rigor.

This is not a hypothetical. In August 2015, a psychologist named Brian Nosek published the answer in Science, and the answer was worse than most researchers expected.

Nosek directed the Center for Open Science at the University of Virginia. He had spent four years organizing the Reproducibility Project, a collaborative effort involving 270 researchers across dozens of institutions on three continents. The premise was simple: take 100 psychology studies published in three top journals, and try to replicate them. Same methods. Same measures. Different labs. See what holds up.

Of the 100 studies, 36 replicated.

Thirty-six percent. In the three most prestigious journals in the field. Studies that had been cited thousands of times. Studies that had been taught in graduate seminars at every major research university. Studies that had formed the empirical backbone of textbooks, TED talks, and popular science books, including several that sit on the same shelf as this one.

The other 64 either failed to replicate entirely or showed effect sizes so much smaller than the originals that the practical significance evaporated. The findings that had shaped careers, launched consulting practices, and informed the advice of a thousand leadership coaches were, in significant number, built on foundations that could not support the weight placed on them.

Nosek did not present the results as an attack on psychology. He presented them as a diagnosis. Science is supposed to be self-correcting. This was the correction.

What Fell

The casualties were not obscure studies from minor labs. They were some of the most famous findings in social psychology, and their collapse sent shockwaves through every field that had borrowed from them.

John Bargh's elderly walking study, published in 1996, had become a textbook example of social priming. Subjects who were exposed to words associated with old age (Florida, wrinkle, bingo) subsequently walked more slowly down the hallway after leaving the lab. The finding was elegant, surprising, and frequently cited. It appeared in Kahneman's *Thinking, Fast and Slow* as evidence for the power of unconscious priming.

In 2012, Stephane Doyen and colleagues at the Universite Libre de Bruxelles attempted a direct replication. They added one element Bargh's original design lacked: the experimenters measuring walking speed did not know which condition the subjects were in. The priming effect vanished. Subsequent replication attempts produced similar results. The elderly walking study, as originally reported, does not hold up. The broader concept of priming has evidence through other pathways, but the flagship experiment that introduced it to the popular imagination is compromised.

Roy Baumeister's ego depletion research, which argued that willpower is a limited resource that depletes with use like a fuel tank, became one of the most cited concepts in self-help and business psychology. The original 1998 study had subjects resist freshly baked cookies and then attempt a difficult puzzle. The cookie-resisters gave up faster. Willpower, Baumeister argued, had been spent.

In 2016, a registered replication report involving 23 laboratories and over 2,000 participants found no evidence for the ego depletion effect. The effect size was essentially zero. The fuel-tank metaphor that had been applied to everything from dieting to corporate decision-making to morning routines had no empirical foundation to stand on.

Amy Cuddy's power posing research, published in 2010, claimed that standing in an expansive posture for two minutes increased testosterone, decreased cortisol, and made subjects more willing to take risks. The finding generated one of the most-viewed TED talks in history, with over 70 million views. In 2016, Cuddy's own co-author, Dana Carney, published a public statement saying she did not believe the effects were real. She listed the specific statistical concerns. Subsequent replications failed to find the hormonal changes. The subjective experience of feeling more powerful has received some partial support in later work, but the biological mechanism that made the original study so striking does not replicate.

Philip Zimbardo's Stanford Prison Experiment, conducted in the basement of Jordan Hall at Stanford in August 1971, had been cited as definitive evidence that situational forces can override individual character. Recent investigations, including reporting by Ben Blum in Medium and research by Thibault Le Texier published in American Psychologist in 2019, revealed that Zimbardo coached the guards, that participants knew they were performing for an audience, and that the "spontaneous" brutality was substantially more directed than the original accounts suggested. The study is not evidence for the power of situations. It is evidence for the power of demand characteristics and experimenter influence.

Each of these studies had been used in books, courses, keynotes, and consulting engagements. Each had been presented to audiences as established science. And each, when subjected to the basic scientific standard of independent replication, either failed or was revealed to be far more limited than advertised.

What Survived

Here is where the story becomes useful rather than depressing.

Not everything fell. Some findings not only survived the replication crisis but emerged stronger, their foundations tested and confirmed across multiple labs, multiple populations, and multiple decades.

The Truth Font (Processing Fluency), the mechanism that opened Part I of this book, is among the most durable findings in cognitive psychology. Reber and Schwarz's 1999 demonstration that easy-to-read statements are judged as more likely to be true has been replicated across languages, cultures, and experimental paradigms. The effect shows up in font studies, in stock market analyses, in restaurant ratings, in political slogans. The underlying mechanism, that the brain uses processing ease as a truth heuristic, is not contested. It is REPLICATED.

The anchoring effect, first demonstrated by Tversky and Kahneman in 1974, has been replicated so extensively that it is now used as a teaching example of a durable finding. The effect holds across professional and novice populations, across cultures, across domains from legal sentencing to real estate pricing to salary negotiations. Judges anchor. Doctors anchor. Experts anchor. The mechanisms debated are the specific cognitive pathways, not the existence of the effect. REPLICATED.

The identifiable victim effect, demonstrated by Small, Loewenstein, and Slovic in 2007, has been replicated across charitable giving contexts, policy support studies, and media analysis. One named person produces more empathy and more action than aggregate statistics. Adding statistics to the individual story reduces response. The finding is consistent and practically significant. REPLICATED.

The mere exposure effect, first established by Robert Zajonc at the University of Michigan in 1968, is one of the most replicated findings in social psychology. Repeated exposure to a stimulus increases liking for that stimulus, even when the exposure occurs below conscious awareness. The effect has been demonstrated with faces, words, musical tones, geometric shapes, and Chinese ideographs shown to non-Chinese speakers. It operates across cultures and age groups. REPLICATED.

Narrative transportation, the tendency for immersive stories to reduce critical evaluation and increase emotional response, was demonstrated by Melanie Green and Timothy Brock at Ohio State University in 2000. It has been replicated across multiple subsequent studies by other researchers. The Commitment and Consistency principle, grounded in Leon Festinger's cognitive dissonance research from the 1950s, has held up across decades of investigation. The Zeigarnik effect, which this book deployed in Chapter 5, has been replicated with some nuance about the conditions that strengthen or weaken it.

The replication crisis did not demolish the science of persuasion. It pruned the dead branches. What remains is stronger for having survived the test.

The Three-Tier System

THE THREE-TIER EVIDENCE SYSTEM

Tier 1

REPLICATED

Core finding independently reproduced

The Truth Font (Reber & Schwarz) • Anchoring (Tversky & Kahneman) • Mere Exposure (Zajonc)

Tier 2

UNCHALLENGED

Published, cited, no failed replication attempts

Narrative Transportation (Green & Brock)
Identifiable Victim (Small et al.)

Tier 3

CONTESTED

Original finding challenged or partially failed replication

Ego Depletion (Baumeister) • Power Posing (Cuddy) • Elderly Walking Priming (Bargh)

This book cites the tier for every study. Chapter 10 explains the system.

This book uses a classification system for every study it cites. The system is transparent because transparency is not just the ethical choice. It is the strategic one.

REPLICATED means the finding has been independently reproduced by researchers other than the original team, in at least one and typically multiple subsequent studies. Processing Fluency is replicated. Anchoring is replicated. The identifiable victim effect is replicated. Mere exposure is replicated. Narrative transportation is replicated. When this book says "the science shows," these are the studies it is leaning on.

UNCHALLENGED means the finding has not been independently replicated but has also not failed replication or been seriously contested. These findings are presented with moderate confidence and a note. A study may be unchallenged because it is too recent for replications to have been attempted, because the experimental design is difficult to reproduce, or because the topic has not attracted replication interest. Unchallenged does not mean weak. It means untested. The BehaviorSec typing-pattern data from Chapter 7 falls in this category: the finding is published and credible, but independent replication by another research group has not been reported.

CONTESTED means the finding has either failed to replicate, produced substantially smaller effect sizes upon replication, or been challenged on methodological grounds by credible researchers. Contested findings are not cited as primary evidence in this book. When they are referenced, the contest is noted explicitly. Power posing is contested. Ego depletion is contested. The Stanford Prison Experiment is contested to the point of disqualification.

This three-tier system is the book's inoculation against the most damaging criticism any nonfiction reader can level: "but that study was debunked." Every reader of business and psychology books has encountered this criticism. They have felt the ground shift under a claim they had built their thinking on. The experience is disorienting and it destroys trust, not just in the specific claim but in the author who presented it without caveat.

This book handles it differently. When a study has been challenged, the challenge is named. When a study has survived replication, the survival is named. The reader is never in the position of discovering, from an outside source, that evidence this book presented as settled is actually contested. That discovery will never happen, because this book got there first.

Why This Matters for AI Content

There is a dimension to the replication crisis that most books in this space do not address, because most books in this space were not built on AI systems.

Large language models are trained on text. That text includes psychology papers, popular science books, TED talk transcripts, and business books that cite the research. The training data does not distinguish between replicated and contested findings. A model that has processed ten thousand references to ego depletion treats it as established fact, because the training data treated it as established fact. The model that generates your marketing copy, your sales page, your email sequence has no mechanism for evaluating whether the psychological principle it is deploying has survived replication or collapsed under scrutiny.

This means AI-generated content that draws on "psychology" is, by default, drawing on a pool that includes contested and failed findings alongside replicated ones. The AI does not know the difference. It cannot know the difference, because replication status is not encoded in the training data as a feature. The model processes "ego depletion" and "anchoring effect" with equal confidence, because both appear with equal frequency in the corpus.

The human architect must be the filter. The three-tier system is not just a credibility tool for the reader. It is an architectural requirement for anyone using AI to deploy cognitive mechanisms. If you instruct an AI to "use the ego depletion principle to structure this email sequence," you are building on a foundation that has already collapsed. If you instruct it to "use the anchoring effect," you are building on bedrock.

The difference is not in the AI's capability. The difference is in the human's knowledge of which science holds up and which does not.

The Inoculation at Work

What this chapter has done to you as a reader is itself a mechanism. And it is worth understanding because it is one of the most powerful credibility tools in the catalog.

In 1961, William McGuire at Yale University proposed a theory of resistance to persuasion that borrowed its metaphor from medicine. A vaccine works by exposing the body to a weakened form of a pathogen. The immune system develops antibodies. When the real pathogen arrives, the body is prepared.

McGuire demonstrated that the same logic applies to beliefs. If you expose someone to a weak version of a counterargument and then refute it, they become more resistant to the full-strength counterargument when they encounter it later. The weakened counterargument is the vaccine. The refutation is the immune response. The subsequent encounter with the real argument finds a prepared mind.

This chapter has inoculated you.

The counterargument against this book is obvious: psychology is in crisis, the studies are unreliable, the principles are built on sand. That argument has power. It is partly true. And you have now been exposed to it, in its strongest form, from the author himself. You have seen which studies fell and why. You have seen which studies survived and why. You have seen the classification system. You are prepared.

When someone at a dinner party, a conference, or in a book review says "but those psychology studies have been debunked," you will not feel the ground shift. You will think: the anchoring effect has been replicated across cultures and professional populations. The Truth Font has survived in every paradigm it has been tested in. The identifiable victim effect has been replicated. The studies that failed are not the ones this framework relies on.

You are inoculated. The antibodies are in place. And the fact that you know you have been inoculated does not reduce the effect. McGuire found that the mechanism operates whether or not the subject is aware of it.

The Architecture of Honest Foundations

This chapter exists because the credibility of everything that follows depends on it. Parts I and II established the CAPTURE and ENGAGE mechanisms. Part III opens with TRUST, and the first two trust mechanisms were the Pratfall Effect (Chapter 9) and the Inoculation Effect (this chapter).

The connection between them is structural. The pratfall earns trust through vulnerability: the author admits a specific, embarrassing failure. The inoculation earns trust through transparency: the author addresses the strongest criticism before the reader encounters it elsewhere. Together, they produce a credibility baseline that is stronger than either could achieve alone.

Consider the alternative. A book that ignored the replication crisis, cited Bargh's priming study and Baumeister's ego depletion without caveat, and presented every finding as equally established would be operating on a credibility fault line. One informed reader, one critical review, one podcast host who asks "but didn't that study fail to replicate?" and the entire foundation cracks. Not just the specific claim. The author's reliability on every claim.

This book chose the other path. Some of these studies failed. That matters. And the studies this book relies on are the ones that survived. That also matters.

The science earns trust through honesty. But science speaks in aggregates. Percentages, effect sizes, replication rates. The brain does not trust aggregates. It trusts one person, with a name, in a specific moment. That is not a weakness. It is the most powerful persuasion mechanism in the catalog.

Deploy It Now (2 minutes)

Find the last piece where you made a claim your audience could challenge. A blog post, a presentation, a chapter draft, a proposal. Look for the strongest objection a smart reader would raise. The real objection, not the easy one.

Now write two sentences before the claim. State the objection. Fairly. Then dismantle it with one specific piece of evidence. "The obvious pushback is [X]. Here is why it does not hold: [specific data or case]."

Read the passage with the inoculation in place. The claim is now harder to attack, because you attacked it first.

McGuire showed in 1961 that pre-exposed counterarguments lose their power. Your reader just got the vaccine.

Chapter 11: One Person's Story Beats a Million Data Points

Scott Harrison was a nightclub promoter in New York City. For ten years, that was the sentence that described his life. He booked venues in the Meatpacking District. He arranged bottle service for hedge fund managers. He got paid to drink Bacardi on camera at sponsored events. By 2004, at age twenty-eight, he was living in a walk-up apartment on the Lower East Side, earning decent money, and feeling a corrosive emptiness that he could not drink or promote his way out of.

He described this later as being "the worst person I knew." Not the most dramatic description. Not the kind of statement that gets standing ovations. But specific, and honest, and from a man who had spent a decade calibrating the reactions of strangers for a living.

Harrison left New York in 2004 and volunteered as a photojournalist aboard the Mercy Ship Anastasis, a floating hospital that provided free surgeries in West Africa. He arrived in Cotonou, Benin, with two suitcases and no plan beyond "stop doing what I was doing." His job was to photograph patients before and after their surgeries. Cleft palates. Tumors that had consumed half a face. Conditions that would have been routine at Mount Sinai but were untreatable in communities where the nearest hospital was three days away.

One patient changed his trajectory.

Her name was not released publicly, but Harrison photographed her before and after a tumor removal surgery. The tumor had been growing on her face for fourteen years. She had not been outside her home in years. In the before photo, she is looking away from the camera. In the after photo, taken weeks later, she is looking directly at it. Smiling.

Harrison returned to New York in 2005 and showed these photos to every person he knew. Not the statistics about 780 million people lacking clean water. Not the aggregate data on preventable disease in Sub-Saharan Africa. The photos. Two photos. One woman. One surgery.

The response stunned him. People who had never given a dollar to international development opened their wallets. Not small checks. Harrison's friends, the same nightclub crowd he had been running with for a decade, donated thousands. One friend who had never expressed a charitable impulse in the years Harrison had known him wrote a check for $15,000 after seeing the two photographs at Harrison's apartment on the Lower East Side, standing in a kitchen that still smelled like last night's takeout.

Harrison noticed something else. The people who donated did not ask for data. They did not ask about the organization's overhead ratio or its programmatic efficiency. They asked about the woman. What was her name? Where was she now? Could they see more photos? The connection was personal. Singular. The woman in the photographs was not a representative of a category. She was herself.

He tested this instinct when he founded Charity: Water in 2006. His first campaigns could have led with the scale of the global water crisis: 780 million people without access to clean water, 3.4 million deaths per year from water-related diseases, entire regions where girls walk six hours a day to collect water instead of attending school. The numbers were staggering. They were also, Harrison suspected, inert.

He led with a person instead. One well. One village. One family. Each campaign opened with a photograph and a name. The donation page showed the face of the person the donation would reach. The follow-up email contained a GPS location and a photo of the completed well.

In the organization's first year, Harrison raised over $1.7 million. His birthday campaigns, where he asked people to donate their birthday to clean water instead of receiving gifts, raised over $70 million in the first ten years. Not through sophisticated marketing infrastructure. Not through data-heavy pitch decks. Through one person at a time, one face at a time, one name at a time.

Meanwhile, organizations with more resources, better data, and more comprehensive messaging strategies were raising less per donor and retaining fewer donors year over year. They had the statistics. They had the annual reports. They had the glossy infographics. Harrison had a photograph of a woman looking at the camera.

The question was not why Harrison's approach worked. That felt obvious to anyone who had seen the photos. The question was why the statistics did not.

Why the Statistics Fail

In 2007, Deborah Small, George Loewenstein, and Paul Slovic at Carnegie Mellon University ran the experiment that answered Harrison's question.

They gave subjects five dollars and asked them to donate to Save the Children. One group received statistical information: food shortages in Malawi affect over three million children. Eleven million people in Ethiopia face immediate food crises. Four million Angolans have been displaced.

The second group received a photograph and a short description of a seven-year-old girl named Rokia from Mali. Rokia was desperately poor. Her family could not reliably feed her. A donation would help provide food and education.

The subjects who read about Rokia gave an average of $2.38. The subjects who read the statistics gave an average of $1.14.

One named girl outperformed three million unnamed children by a factor of two.

But the experiment had a third condition. And this is where the finding turns from interesting to alarming. The third group received both: Rokia's story AND the statistics. The combined group gave $1.43. Less than the Rokia-only group by a significant margin.

Adding statistics to the individual story did not boost donations. It reduced them.

The data diluted the empathy.

Slovic called this the "collapse of compassion." When the brain processes aggregate numbers, it shifts from empathetic processing to analytical processing. The analytical mode is cooler, more detached, and less generous. The individual story activates the heart. The statistic activates the calculator. And the calculator is stingy.

The Operating Logic of Human Empathy

The identifiable victim effect is not a quirk. It is the operating logic of human empathy.

The brain's empathy system evolved for face-to-face interactions in small groups. It is optimized for one person at a time. One face. One name. One story. When someone describes a single individual in need, the medial prefrontal cortex and the anterior insula activate. These are the regions associated with empathetic concern and emotional simulation. The brain models the individual's experience. It feels something.

When someone describes a million people in need, those regions do not activate proportionally. They do not activate at all in many cases. A million is not a million individual experiences to the brain. It is a number. An abstraction. The brain cannot feel a million. It can feel one.

Slovic wrote about this in a 2007 paper that has shaped the field: "The more who die, the less we care." Not because people are callous. Because the empathy system has bandwidth limitations. It was built for the village, not the globe.

This is not a flaw the reader should try to overcome. It is a mechanism the reader should deploy.

The Surgeon's Story That Changed Hospital Policy

Charity: Water is not the only domain where the identifiable victim effect has driven outsized change. Consider the case of Atul Gawande, a surgeon at Brigham and Women's Hospital in Boston.

By 2007, the aggregate data on medical errors in American hospitals was well established. The Institute of Medicine had published "To Err Is Human" in 1999, estimating that medical errors caused between 44,000 and 98,000 deaths per year in the United States. The number was cited in academic journals, in congressional testimony, in hospital board meetings across the country. It was known. And for eight years, the aggregate data had produced almost no systemic change in surgical safety protocols.

Gawande changed the conversation with a story.

In December 2007, he published "The Checklist" in The New Yorker. The article opens with a three-year-old girl in a small town in the Austrian Alps. She had fallen into an icy fishpond near her family's home. By the time her parents found her, she had been submerged in near-freezing water long enough that the paramedics who arrived on scene found no pulse and no breathing. Her core body temperature had dropped to 66 degrees. By all conventional measures, she was dead.

Gawande does not describe the rescue as a single heroic act. He describes it as a cascade of decisions, each one dependent on the last, any one of which could fail. The emergency team needed to place her on a heart-lung bypass machine to warm her blood gradually without causing cardiac arrhythmia. Surgeons needed to repair the damage that prolonged oxygen deprivation had caused. A series of precise, sequential interventions, each one invisible to anyone outside the operating room, each one dependent on someone making the right call at the right moment.

The girl lived. Her neurological function recovered nearly to baseline. Gawande uses her survival not as a triumph but as an illustration of how close the system comes to failure, how many individual steps must go right, and how little infrastructure exists to ensure that they do.

The article produced something the aggregate data had not: urgency. Within months, the World Health

Organization launched a global surgical safety checklist initiative. Peter Pronovost's earlier checklist work at Johns Hopkins, which had been producing impressive results in ICU settings (a 66 percent reduction in central-line infections, saving an estimated 1,500 lives and $100 million over 18 months in Michigan alone) but struggling to gain institutional adoption outside of the ICU community, suddenly had momentum. Hospitals that had been aware of the data for years began implementing the protocols.

The data had been available for eight years. One surgeon's story about one patient moved the system. The same mechanism explains why public health campaigns that feature one named patient with a specific story outperform campaigns citing aggregate mortality statistics.

Gawande did not ignore the data. He placed it after the story. The individual case created the emotional engagement. The aggregate data provided the intellectual justification. But the order was not interchangeable. Data first would have produced another report that sat on another shelf. Story first produced a movement.

The Uncomfortable Lesson for Data People

You have done the opposite.

You have stood in front of a room with a slide deck full of numbers and wondered why no one reacted. You have written a report dense with evidence and watched it collect dust in a shared drive. You have crafted the perfect statistical argument and watched a competitor win the account with a single customer testimonial.

The instinct of the analytically trained mind is to start with the data. The data is the evidence. The data is the proof. Starting with a story feels unserious, manipulative, soft. It feels like you are cheating.

You are not cheating. You are working with the brain you are trying to reach, not against it. The individual story is not a decoration on the data. It is the delivery mechanism through which the data enters the brain's processing system in a form the brain can act on. Data without a delivery mechanism produces awareness. A story with data produces action.

Harrison understood this. Every Charity: Water campaign begins with one person. One name. One situation. The data follows. But the donor has already committed before the data arrives, because the brain committed to Rokia before it had a chance to calculate.

What Changed When I Led with a Person

I discovered this mechanism the hard way, in my own content.

In the early months of the AI publishing system, I wrote book descriptions for Amazon the way most authors write them: summary of contents, credentials of the author, bullet points of what the reader would learn. The descriptions were accurate. They were professional. They performed the way Karen Blackwell's campaign performed: within norms. Forgettable.

Then I tested the identifiable victim effect. Same book. Same audience targeting. Same ad spend. Two descriptions. Version A opened with "In this groundbreaking book, you will learn the 46 cognitive mechanisms that drive human decisions." Version B opened with "Sarah Chen spent four months building a marketing campaign that failed in eight days. She had the data. She had the talent. She was missing something she couldn't name."

Version B outperformed Version A by 2.4x in click-through rate to the book's sales page. The conversion from page view to purchase was nearly identical for both groups once they reached the page. The entire difference was at the top of the funnel. The named person opened the door. The benefits walked through it.

I ran the same test across email subject lines. Subject lines that opened with a person's name and a specific situation ("How a product manager at Stripe discovered..." or "The mistake a Shopify founder made on the first day") outperformed benefit-oriented subject lines ("Learn the 3 strategies that...") by an average of 37 percent in open rates across a sample of 4,200 sends over eight weeks.

The pattern was consistent enough that it became a rule in the system. Every piece of content now leads with a person. Not as a stylistic preference. As an architectural requirement.

Deployment Across Three Modes

In narrative mode, the protagonist IS the identifiable victim mechanism. Every fiction reader bonds with one character. Not with a group. Not with a cause. One person whose name they know, whose fears they share, whose victories they need. The protagonist does for fiction what Rokia does for charitable giving: creates a singular emotional connection that carries the entire experience.

In argument mode, the identifiable victim is the chapter opening. Every chapter in this book opens with a named person in a specific moment. Not because it is a nice storytelling convention. Because the brain cannot engage with abstractions until it has engaged with an individual. The named person opens the door. The principle walks through it. Gawande did not explain the checklist and then offer a patient story as illustration. He put you in the operating room first. The checklist became necessary because you had already met the patient whose life depended on it.

In commercial mode, the identifiable victim is the customer testimonial with a name and a specific story. Not "Our customers love us." Not a Net Promoter Score. One customer. One name. One sentence about what changed for them. "Before Basecamp, our project updates were scattered across twelve email threads. Now they are in one place. We shipped two weeks early for the first time in three years." That testimonial outperforms aggregate satisfaction data because the brain processes one person's experience through the empathy system and a thousand ratings through the calculator.

For B2B marketing, the deployment is identical. The case study that names the company, the decision-maker, and the specific problem converts at a higher rate than the white paper that describes industry trends. For fundraising, the deployment is what Harrison built Charity: Water on. For political communication, the deployment is why every State of the Union address puts a named person in the gallery. For journalism, the deployment is why ProPublica opened their algorithmic bias investigation with Brisha Borden, not with a statistical analysis of risk scores across racial demographics.

The deployment pattern is the same across all three modes: the individual first. The data second. Always.

The Paradox of Scale

There is something uncomfortable about the identifiable victim effect. It means that the scale of a problem does not predict the response to it. Three million children in food crisis produce less action than one seven-year-old girl named Rokia. This is not rational. It is not fair. It is how the brain works.

The communicator who understands this mechanism does not lament it. They deploy it.

One named customer beats a thousand anonymous reviews. One case study with a name and a timeline and a specific outcome beats a page of statistics. One employee's story about how the new process changed their workday beats a 47-slide deck about organizational efficiency gains.

The person comes first. The data comes second. And the person must have a name.

The identifiable victim earns trust through empathy. The replication chapter earned trust through honesty. The pratfall earned trust through vulnerability. Together, they accomplish the TRUST job. But trust is not desire. The reader who trusts you has not decided to act. For that, you need something that feels dangerous. Something that triggers the oldest autonomy drive in the human brain.

Deploy It Now (90 seconds)

Find the last piece you wrote that leads with a statistic, a percentage, or an aggregate claim. A case study that opens with industry data. An article that starts with "Organizations that do X see a Y% increase."

Now rewrite the opening sentence. Replace the aggregate with one person. Give them a name, a role, and a specific situation. "Sarah, a product manager at a

40-person company, spent three weeks on a launch that produced eleven signups." Then let the statistic follow.

Read both versions. The version with Sarah pulls harder. That is the Identifiable Victim Effect. Small, Loewenstein, and Slovic measured it in 2007. The brain cannot feel a percentage. It can feel one person.

Chapter 12: The Freedom You Can't Have

In 1966, a psychologist named Jack Brehm at Duke University set up an experiment that was almost comically simple. He showed subjects a set of consumer products and asked them to rate how much they wanted each one. Then he told them that one of the products was not available. They could not have it.

Brehm measured their desire again.

The product they could not have was now the product they wanted most. Not by a small margin. The restriction had transformed a moderately desirable item into the most desired item in the set. Nothing about the product had changed. Nothing about the other options had changed. The only thing that had changed was the freedom to choose it.

Brehm called this psychological reactance — what I call **The Velvet Rope**. The theory is straightforward: when a freedom is threatened or eliminated, people experience a motivational state directed toward restoring that freedom. The threatened freedom becomes more attractive. The restriction does not reduce desire. It creates it.

This is not a subtle effect. And it is not limited to consumer products.

When Miami-Dade County banned the use of phosphate-based laundry detergents in 1973, researchers Michael Mazis, Robert Settle, and Dennis Leslie surveyed residents on both sides of the county line. Residents in the county where the detergent was banned rated the banned product as gentler, more effective, and better overall than residents in adjacent counties where the same product was freely available. The product was identical. The chemistry had not changed. The ban had made it better.

The brain does not evaluate restricted options on their merits. It evaluates them on their scarcity. And scarcity, manufactured or real, is one of the most reliable desire generators in the architecture.

The $32 T-Shirt That Costs $300

James Jebbia opened the first Supreme store at 274 Lafayette Street in downtown Manhattan in April 1994. The space was small. Twelve hundred square feet. The product selection was limited. The branding was deliberately confrontational: a red box logo that borrowed its font from Barbara Kruger's political art, slapped onto skateboards, T-shirts, and hoodies.

For the first decade, Supreme was a downtown skate shop with a cult following. The merchandise was not expensive. A logo T-shirt retailed for $32. A hoodie for around $138. The quality was solid but unremarkable. What was remarkable was the business model that Jebbia refined over the following twenty years.

Supreme does not sell products. Supreme restricts access to products.

The "drop" model works like this: Supreme releases a limited quantity of new items every Thursday at 11:00 AM. Online and in-store. When the items sell out, they are gone. There is no restock. There is no waitlist. There is no "coming back in your size next week." You are either there at 11:00 AM or you are not. The product you missed is the product you cannot have.

By 2017, Supreme was generating over $500 million in annual revenue. In November 2020, VF Corporation acquired the brand for $2.1 billion. A $32 T-shirt sold on the resale market for $300 or more. Sometimes much more. A Supreme brick, a literal clay brick with the logo stamped on it, retailed for $30 and resold for $150.

The question every traditional marketer asks about Supreme is: why? The products are not superior. The designs are not complex. The materials are not exceptional. What justifies a 10x premium on a T-shirt?

Brehm answered that question in 1966, thirty years before Jebbia opened his store. The restriction IS the value. Every sold-out drop is a freedom eliminated. Every missed Thursday at 11:00 AM is a choice the consumer can no longer make. Reactance converts the restriction into desire. The desire converts into willingness to pay. The willingness to pay converts into a $2.1 billion valuation for a brand that sells, at its core, the experience of not being able to buy what you want.

The Mechanism Nobody Admits They Fall For

Reactance is the mechanism that people deny most and fall for most reliably.

Tell someone they cannot do something and watch what happens. "You probably should not read this section until you have finished Chapter 13." You are still reading. "This framework is not for everyone." You want it more. "I was not going to include this case study." You need to hear it.

The mechanism operates pre-consciously. By the time the reader is aware they want the restricted option more, the desire has already been manufactured. The conscious mind produces a rationalization: "I want it because it is good, not because it is scarce." The rationalization is itself evidence that reactance has fired. If the desire were truly about quality, the restriction would be irrelevant.

You have experienced this in contexts that have nothing to do with shopping. A friend tells you not to look at something. You look. A colleague mentions a meeting you were not invited to. You want to know what happened in that meeting. A news article is paywalled. You consider subscribing for the first time.

The restriction does not need to be absolute. Even partial restrictions trigger reactance. "Only available until Friday." "Limited to the first 200." "For members only." Each of these statements performs the same cognitive operation: it tells the brain that a freedom is about to be removed, and the brain responds by wanting to exercise that freedom before it disappears.

When Reactance Backfires

Brehm's theory includes a condition that most marketers ignore: reactance is strongest when the freedom was previously available and is now being removed, AND when the person believes they are entitled to that freedom.

This means reactance can be deployed badly.

When Coca-Cola replaced its original formula with New Coke in April 1985, the company triggered one of the largest reactance events in consumer history. Customers had been drinking Classic Coke for ninety-nine years. It was freely available. They were entitled to it. The removal of that freedom produced outrage so intense that Coca-Cola reversed the decision within seventy-nine days.

The company received over 400,000 letters and phone calls. People were not angry about the taste. Blind taste tests showed many preferred New Coke. They were angry about the restriction. Their freedom to choose the original had been eliminated without their consent.

The lesson is not that reactance is dangerous. The lesson is that reactance must be deployed with precision. Supreme restricts access to a new product the consumer has never had. That triggers desire. Coca-Cola restricted access to an existing product the consumer had always had. That triggers rage.

The distinction is between creating scarcity for something new and removing access to something established. One builds a brand worth $2.1 billion. The other nearly destroys a brand worth far more.

The Status Quo Has a Price Tag

Reactance is one of three WANT mechanisms this chapter deploys. The second is what I call **The Comfortable Prison**.

Before presenting a new approach, the architecture requires making the cost of the current approach visible. Not abstract cost. Concrete, specific, felt cost. The brain defaults to the status quo because the status quo feels safe. Making its price tag visible disrupts that default.

The average B2B company spends $92,000 per year on content marketing. Of the content produced, 60 to 70 percent goes entirely unused by sales teams, according to SiriusDecisions research from 2018. Not underperforming. Unused. Sitting in a shared drive, never opened, never downloaded, never shared with a prospect. That is $55,000 to $64,000 spent on content nobody reads.

Think about what $55,000 buys. It buys a full-time junior copywriter for a year. It buys 550 hours of freelance writing at $100 an hour. It buys enough ad spend to test forty different landing pages against each other and find the one that converts. Instead, it buys blog posts that sit in folders with names like "Q3-Content-Assets-FINAL-v3" and download counts of zero.

The content is not bad. It is architecturally empty. It captures attention and does nothing with it. It lists features without creating cognitive gaps. It presents data without leading with an identifiable victim. It closes with "contact us for a demo" without deploying a completion impulse or reducing the first step to something the brain cannot refuse.

The reader who has been nodding along for eleven chapters knows why this content fails. They can name the missing mechanisms. And they are beginning to realize that their own content may be part of the $55,000.

I ran an audit on my own system that confirmed the pattern. Before I built the Influence Architecture framework into the AI agents' instructions, the marketing content the system produced had the same profile: competent prose, zero architectural deployment. Email open rates were in the 18 to 22 percent range. Landing page conversion sat at 1.1 percent. Within industry norms. Respectable. The status quo.

After I restructured the agents' instructions around the six cognitive jobs, open rates moved to 28 to 34 percent. Landing page conversion moved to 2.8 percent. The content itself was not dramatically better in any way a casual reader would notice. But the architecture was present. Each email accomplished a specific cognitive job. Each landing page deployed a minimum of four mechanisms. The status quo had been costing me roughly 40 percent of the conversion rate the architecture delivered, and I did not know until I stopped accepting the status quo as normal.

Motivated Reasoning as an Ally

The third WANT mechanism is Motivated Reasoning Judo.

Motivated reasoning is the brain's tendency to evaluate evidence through the lens of what the person already wants to believe. Ziva Kunda documented this in her 1990 paper "The Case for Motivated Reasoning," published in Psychological Bulletin. Kunda showed that people generate and evaluate arguments in a biased fashion, favoring conclusions they want to reach, but only within the bounds of what they can justify to themselves. The bias is real, robust, and replicated across decades of research. It is usually discussed as a flaw to overcome. In the architecture, it is a force to redirect.

The reader of this book is motivated to see themselves as serious about their craft, ahead of the curve, deeper than the popular sources. That motivation is not a problem. It is an engine.

When this book says "Cialdini identified seven principles; this framework catalogs forty-six," the reader's motivated reasoning does not resist the claim. It embraces it. The reader WANTS the more complete framework because the more complete framework confirms their identity as someone who goes deeper than most. They are not being sold. They are being seen.

This is Motivated Reasoning Judo: instead of fighting the reader's existing identity commitments, aligning the new information with those commitments. The reader who sees themselves as sophisticated wants the sophisticated framework. The reader who sees themselves as contrarian wants the framework the mainstream has not discovered yet. The reader who sees themselves as a practitioner wants the framework that includes deployment instructions, not just theory.

The judo move is framing. Not "here is what you should believe." But "here is what the practitioners who take this seriously already know." The reader's identity does the rest.

Patagonia ran the cleanest commercial demonstration of this mechanism in the Black Friday print ad that ran in the New York Times on November 25, 2011. The headline read: "Don't Buy This Jacket." Underneath was a full-page image of their best-selling R2 fleece, with a list of the environmental costs of producing it, including the 135 liters of water required even though the jacket was made from 60 percent recycled material. On the most retail-aggressive day of the year, the company that makes the jacket told readers not to buy it. Sales grew roughly 36 percent the following year, from $400 million in 2011 to $543 million in 2012. The ad did not argue against consumption. It rode the reader's existing identity as an environmentally conscious person and showed them that Patagonia shared that identity. Motivated reasoning did the rest. A reader who believed "I am the kind of person who thinks about the planet" did not have their belief challenged. They had their belief recognized, by a brand that had just demonstrated willingness to forfeit a sale to honor it. The purchase followed, because the purchase now meant something aligned with who the reader already wanted to be.

Notice what the ad did not do. It did not say "we are the virtuous choice" (a brand claim the reader would have to evaluate). It did not say "buy our products because they are better for the environment" (a conclusion the reader would have to accept). It said something the reader could confirm independently: here are the costs of this jacket, and only buy it if you truly need it. The reader supplied the rest of the argument themselves. That is the judo. The brand did not push; the reader's own motivation pulled.

The mechanism has a failure mode that needs to be named, because it is easy to mistake for the real thing. Motivated Reasoning Judo is not flattery. Flattery tells the reader that they already believe the correct things and therefore should agree with whatever comes next. The reader notices. Flattery triggers the same suspicion as any unearned compliment. A political candidate who tells voters "the real Americans know the truth, and I am speaking to you" is attempting judo but performing flattery. The reader who does not share the identity being flattered tunes out. The reader who does share it registers the pandering.

The distinction is that real judo starts from something the reader can verify in the material itself, not from an identity claim the author asserts. Patagonia did not tell environmentally conscious readers they were environmentally conscious. Patagonia showed them production data and then trusted them to draw the conclusion their existing identity already supported. This book does not tell the reader they are a serious practitioner. It shows the reader forty-six mechanisms, some of which they had not seen before, and trusts that a serious practitioner will recognize the distance between instinct and architecture as a distance worth closing.

The judo is never the author's claim about the reader's identity. The judo is always the material the reader evaluates through the lens of the identity they already brought to the page.

AI systems can deploy this same alignment with remarkable precision. An AI that understands the target reader's identity profile can frame every claim, every case study, every deployment instruction to align with that identity. Not by changing the content. By matching the frame to the motivation. The same factual claim about The Truth Font, framed for a data-driven reader ("the effect size was 0.47 across four replications"), for a creative reader ("the sentence that feels inevitable on the page is the one the brain trusts"), or for a contrarian reader ("this is the mechanism most advertising professionals have never heard of") is three deployments of the same science. The AI can select the frame. The human decides the identity to target. The judo is automated.

The risk in automated deployment is the flattery failure mode at scale. An AI that optimizes purely for identity alignment will drift toward pandering, because pandering produces measurable short-term engagement. The calibration that prevents the drift is the same one a careful human author uses: show the material; trust the identity already in the room to interpret it; never tell the reader who they are.

What Desire Actually Looks Like in Architecture

Three mechanisms. Reactance. Status quo disruption. Motivated reasoning alignment. Together, they compose the WANT job.

Reactance creates desire by restricting access. The reader wants what they are told they cannot have. The chapter title did this: "The Freedom You Can't Have" is a restriction masquerading as a heading. You opened this chapter partly because you were told you could not have something.

Status quo disruption creates desire by making inaction expensive. The reader learns that their current approach has a specific, measurable cost. The comfortable default stops feeling comfortable.

Motivated reasoning alignment creates desire by connecting the new framework to the reader's existing identity. The reader does not change who they are. They become more of who they already are. The framework is the tool that closes the gap between the person they think they are and the person they want to be.

In commercial mode, these three mechanisms compose the section of a sales page between the problem statement and the call to action. The product is restricted (limited enrollment, closing soon, not for everyone). The current approach is costly (you are spending $55,000 on content nobody reads). The product aligns with the reader's identity (for practitioners who take this seriously).

In narrative mode, these mechanisms compose Act Two of any story. The protagonist wants something. The want is intensified by a restriction (the mentor says no, the object is guarded, the opportunity is closing). The status quo becomes untenable (the consequences of not acting are shown). The protagonist's identity aligns with action (this is who I am, this is what I do).

In argument mode, which is where you are standing right now, these mechanisms compose the section of the book where understanding shifts to motivation. You trusted the science. You understood the mechanisms. And now you want to deploy them. The restriction is that you cannot deploy all forty-six by instinct. The status quo is costing you results you can measure. Your identity as a serious practitioner demands the architecture.

Reactance creates desire by restricting access. But there is a deeper form of desire, one that does not trigger when something is scarce but when something becomes part of who you are.

Deploy It Now (90 seconds)

Find the last piece where you described something as available, open, or accessible to everyone. A product page, a course listing, a workshop registration, a newsletter signup.

Now add one real constraint. A deadline, a capacity limit, a qualification. Not a lie. A real boundary.

"Join the course" becomes "12 seats left in the March cohort." "Download the guide" becomes "Available until Friday." "Book a call" becomes "I take 4 new clients per quarter." "Register for the workshop" becomes "We cap enrollment at 20."

Read both versions. The version with the constraint creates a pull the open version does not. That pull is Reactance. Brehm measured it in 1966. Your reader feels it in 2026.

Chapter 13: You Are What You Buy

In 2007, Jonah Berger and Chip Heath at Stanford University published a study that most marketers have never read and that explains the single most important thing about why people recommend books.

Berger and Heath were studying identity signaling: the way people use consumer choices to communicate who they are to others. The specific question they asked was not why people adopt products. It was why people abandon them. What makes someone stop wearing a brand, stop quoting a phrase, stop recommending a book they once loved?

The answer was contamination.

Berger and Heath ran a series of experiments in which a product or cultural preference became associated with an out-group. In one study, students at Stanford were given Livestrong-style rubber bracelets. The bracelets were popular. Students wore them freely. Then Berger and Heath introduced the same bracelets to a group the Stanford students did not want to be associated with: "geeky" academic departments (their framing, not mine). When the out-group adopted the bracelets, the original group stopped wearing them. Not because the bracelets had changed. Because the identity signal had changed.

The product was the same object. But a product is never just an object. It is a signal. It says something about the person who uses it, wears it, reads it, recommends it. And when the signal no longer communicates the desired identity, the product is abandoned, regardless of its intrinsic quality.

This finding is not limited to rubber bracelets. It explains why people recommend certain books and not others, why some frameworks enter the cultural vocabulary and others disappear, and why the most commercially valuable thing this book can give you is not information. It is language.

The Gift That Recommends Itself

There is a specific category of intellectual product that generates its own marketing. Not through advertising. Not through algorithms. Through the act of being used.

Carol Dweck, a psychologist at Stanford, published *Mindset: The New Psychology of Success* in 2006. The book introduced a distinction between a "fixed mindset" (the belief that intelligence and talent are static) and a "growth mindset" (the belief that they can be developed). The academic research behind growth mindset has been contested. Replication studies have found effect sizes much smaller than Dweck originally reported. The educational interventions based on the theory have produced mixed results.

And none of that has mattered commercially.

"Growth mindset" as a phrase has become cultural infrastructure. Teachers use it in classrooms. Managers use it in performance reviews. Parents use it at dinner tables. Satya Nadella restructured Microsoft's internal culture around it, describing the shift in his 2017 book *Hit Refresh*. The phrase appears in job descriptions, in conference keynotes, in coaching conversations. It has been cited in over 10,000 academic papers. The vocabulary outlived the academic debate about the research.

This is the Vocabulary Gift. When you give someone a word for something they have always experienced but never articulated, you give them a tool they will use for the rest of their life. And every time they use that word, they recommend the source they learned it from.

"Sunk cost fallacy." People threw good money after bad for centuries. Then the term entered common vocabulary, and suddenly millions of people had a name for the pattern. Each use of the phrase is a tiny, unconscious advertisement for the discipline of behavioral economics. "Imposter syndrome." Millions of accomplished professionals felt like frauds. Pauline Clance and Suzanne Imes named the pattern in 1978. Now when someone says "I think I have imposter syndrome," they are using a vocabulary gift. The phrase carries its origin with it.

Nassim Nicholas Taleb coined "antifragile" in 2012 to describe systems that get stronger under stress. The concept existed before the word. Stoic philosophers had described it. Engineers had observed it. But the word made the concept portable. "That organization is antifragile" is a sentence people say in meetings. Each time they say it, someone asks: "What does that mean?" And the answer is a book recommendation.

The mechanism is what I call **The Badge** — identity signaling in its purest form. The person who uses the vocabulary is not just communicating information. They are communicating: I am the kind of person who reads this kind of book, who thinks at this level, who has access to this framework. The vocabulary is a badge. And badges are displayed.

The Six Words You Have Already Started Using

This book has been giving you vocabulary gifts since Chapter 1.

CAPTURE. ENGAGE. TRUST. WANT. ACT. BOND.

Six cognitive jobs. Six words. If you have read this far, you have already internalized them. You could, right now, look at a landing page and say: "The CAPTURE is fine, but the TRUST job is empty. There is no credibility signal in the first scroll." You could sit in a meeting where someone presents a content strategy and think: "This handles ENGAGE but skips straight to ACT without building WANT." You could evaluate an email campaign and identify which jobs it accomplishes and which it misses.

You have been using the vocabulary before this chapter named the mechanism.

That was not accidental. The architecture of this book introduced the six cognitive jobs in Chapter 1 as an organizational tool. Each subsequent chapter taught mechanisms grouped by job. The reader absorbed the vocabulary through use, the same way children absorb language: not through memorization but through immersion. By Chapter 5, CAPTURE and ENGAGE were intuitive categories. By Chapter 10, TRUST had earned its meaning through three chapters of deployment. Now, at Chapter 13, you are not learning the vocabulary. You are recognizing that you already own it.

The moment you give someone a word for something they have always felt but never articulated, you have given them a tool they will use for the rest of their life. And every time they use that word, they recommend the book they learned it from.

How the Vocabulary Enters the Room

Consider what happens when you leave this book and return to your work.

You sit in a meeting on a Tuesday morning. Someone presents a campaign. The landing page is open on the screen. The design is clean. The copy is professional. It lists features, quotes a testimonial, and ends with a "Get Started" button.

Before reading this book, you would have said: "Looks good. Maybe tweak the headline."

Now you see something different. The CAPTURE is adequate: the headline interrupts. But there is no ENGAGE mechanism. Nothing creates a cognitive gap. Nothing poses a question the visitor needs answered. The page lists benefits without making the visitor feel the cost of NOT having the product. There is no WANT. The CTA is a four-word button, which handles The Truth Font, but nothing before it has built the desire that makes clicking feel inevitable.

You say: "The CAPTURE is fine, but we are skipping from CAPTURE to ACT. There is no ENGAGE. There is no WANT. We are asking people to act before we have given their brain a reason to want it."

The room pauses. Someone asks what you mean by CAPTURE and WANT. You explain. You are not reciting a book. You are using a diagnostic vocabulary that happens to be portable, precise, and immediately useful. The explanation takes ninety seconds. At the end of it, the person who asked has a new way to evaluate every landing page they will ever see.

That ninety-second explanation is a book recommendation that does not sound like a book recommendation. It sounds like expertise. And the next time that person encounters a poorly structured campaign, they will reach for the same vocabulary. CAPTURE, ENGAGE, TRUST, WANT, ACT, BOND. Six words. Each one a handle. Each handle a recommendation.

AI systems amplify this effect. An AI agent instructed to use the six cognitive job names consistently across all marketing output, all email copy, all internal briefs, all editorial calendars, creates a shared vocabulary layer across every touchpoint a brand produces. The framework names become the organization's native language for evaluating communication. Not because a memo mandated adoption. Because the vocabulary works. It names something people needed named. And once named, it cannot be unnamed.

Identity Signaling as Architecture

Berger and Heath's research reveals the mechanism behind the vocabulary gift: identity signaling. Every word you use signals membership in a group. When you say "sunk cost fallacy," you signal that you belong to the group of people who think in terms of cognitive biases. When you say "growth mindset," you signal that you value learning over fixed performance. When you say "CAPTURE" to describe the first job a piece of content must do, you signal something specific: I understand the architecture of influence at a level most people do not.

The signal is the marketing.

This is why frameworks with memorable names generate disproportionate commercial returns. Cialdini's six principles (before he added a seventh) are remembered because they have names: reciprocity, commitment, social proof, authority, liking, scarcity. Each name is a handle the reader grabs in conversation. Miller's "StoryBrand" works commercially because the name itself is portable. "We need to StoryBrand our messaging" is a sentence that generates consulting revenue every time it is spoken.

The identity mechanism explains a pattern that confuses people who think about influence in terms of quality alone. A book with better research but less memorable vocabulary will underperform a book with good-enough research and brilliant naming. This is not a flaw in the marketplace. It is the identity signaling mechanism operating as designed. The brain selects for portable vocabulary because portable vocabulary lets the user signal membership in a desirable group. The vocabulary IS the value proposition.

The Worldview Lens

There is a level above the vocabulary gift. It is the rarest and most commercially valuable intellectual product a nonfiction author can create.

Kahneman gave readers "System 1 and System 2." After reading Thinking, Fast and Slow, a certain kind of reader could not evaluate a decision without asking: is this my System 1 or my System 2? The framework became a perceptual lens. Not a tool the reader picks up and puts down. A filter the reader sees through permanently.

Taleb gave readers "antifragile." After reading the book, a certain kind of reader evaluated every system they encountered for its response to stress. Does this get stronger or weaker under pressure? The lens was installed.

Clayton Christensen gave readers "disruption." The word existed before him. But after *The Innovator's Dilemma,* "disruption" as Christensen defined it became a perceptual filter. Is this company being disrupted? Is this market vulnerable to disruption from below? The lens changed what people saw.

Each of these frameworks shares four properties.

First, it has a memorable name. Two to three words. Short enough to use in conversation. Specific enough to mean something precise.

Second, it works across multiple domains. System 1 and System 2 apply to personal decisions, corporate strategy, and public policy. Antifragile applies to biology, finance, and organizational design. A framework that works in only one domain is a tool. A framework that works in three domains is a lens.

Third, it creates a self-recognition moment. The reader catches themselves applying the lens without being prompted. They are reading the newspaper and think: "That is a System 1 error." They are in a meeting and think: "This organization is fragile." The lens has been installed when it operates automatically.

Fourth, it provides social vocabulary. The reader can say "that is a System 1 problem" in a meeting and be understood by others who have read the book. The vocabulary creates a community of shared perception. And every conversation within that community is an unpaid marketing event.

What This Book Is Installing

The Influence Architecture framework is designed to meet all four criteria.

The name is portable. "Influence Architecture" is a phrase you can use in conversation. "That campaign has an Architecture Gap" is a sentence that communicates a specific diagnosis and signals a specific level of understanding.

The framework works across three modes. Narrative, argument, and commercial. The same forty-six mechanisms deploy in fiction writing, in nonfiction argument, and in marketing. A reader who learns the framework for their email campaigns will start seeing it in the novels they read and the political speeches they watch. The cross-domain applicability is what converts a catalog into a lens.

The self-recognition moment has already begun. You are reading case studies in this book and tagging the mechanisms before the chapter names them. That is the lens operating. You saw The Truth Font in the Reber and Schwarz experiment before Chapter 2 named it. You felt The Open Loop in Chapter 5 before you understood why you could not stop reading. You recognized the Pratfall Effect in Chapter 9 before the chapter explained why the author's failure increased your trust.

The social vocabulary is the six cognitive jobs: CAPTURE, ENGAGE, TRUST, WANT, ACT, BOND. Plus the mechanism names: The Truth Font, The Open Loop, Commitment Escalation, the Identifiable Victim Effect. Each name is a conversational tool. Each tool, when used, carries this book into the conversation.

The moment you give someone a word for something they have always felt but never articulated, you have given them a tool they will use for the rest of their life. And every time they use that word, they recommend the book they learned it from.

The Identity You Are Building

Berger and Heath found that people adopt products that signal desirable group membership and abandon products that become associated with undesirable groups. The inverse is also true: people seek out products, books, and frameworks that help them become the person they want to be.

The reader who finishes this book is not the same reader who started it. Not because the information has changed them. Because the vocabulary has changed how they see. They sit in meetings and identify missing cognitive jobs. They read sales pages and tag the mechanisms. They watch advertisements and see the architecture.

They have become the person who sees the architecture.

That identity is self-reinforcing. The more they use the vocabulary, the more it becomes part of how they think. The more it becomes part of how they think, the more they use it. And every time they use it, they strengthen both the identity and the book's reach.

This is not manipulation. It is the honest consequence of building a framework with memorable names and cross-domain applicability. Cialdini did it with six principles. Kahneman did it with two systems. Dweck did it with two mindsets. Each of these authors gave readers a perceptual lens that the reader chose to install because the lens was genuinely useful.

The architecture you have been learning is genuinely useful. The vocabulary is genuinely portable. The question is no longer whether you understand the framework. You do. The question is whether you will deploy it.

Identity creates desire. Vocabulary creates transmission. But desire alone does not produce action. For that, you need something more uncomfortable. You need to make NOT acting more painful than acting.

Deploy It Now (2 minutes)

Open the last piece where you described a problem your audience faces. A landing page, a video script, a presentation slide, a newsletter, a lesson plan.

Look for the place where you explained the problem in a full sentence or paragraph. Now replace the explanation with a name. Two or three words that label the pattern. Not jargon. A phrase your audience could use at dinner: "That is a [your term] problem."

Test it: could your reader say that phrase in a meeting and have a colleague ask, "What do you mean by that?" If yes, you have built a Vocabulary Gift. Every time they use that phrase, they carry your framework into the conversation. Dweck did it with "growth mindset." Taleb did it with "antifragile." Your version starts with naming the thing your audience feels but cannot yet articulate.

Chapter 14: The Price of Doing Nothing

You have been nodding along for thirteen chapters.

You agreed with every premise. You found the evidence credible. You recognized yourself in the case studies. You built a mental model of the architecture, piece by piece, and not once did you put the book down and think: this is wrong.

Here is the cost of that agreement.

You now hold a belief that contradicts your behavior. You believe the architecture works. You believe that deploying three or four mechanisms by instinct is categorically inferior to deploying forty-six by design. You believe the evidence. And you have not changed a single thing about how you create content.

That contradiction has a name. In 1959, Leon Festinger and James Carlsmith at Stanford University designed an experiment to study it.

They paid subjects to do something boring and then lie about it. The task was genuinely tedious. Subjects spent an hour turning wooden pegs on a board, one quarter turn at a time. Monotonous, repetitive, pointless. After the hour, the experimenter made a request: a research assistant had failed to show up, and the subject was asked to tell the next participant that the task was enjoyable and interesting. To lie.

One group was paid $20 for the lie. Another group was paid $1.

Then both groups were asked to rate how much they had actually enjoyed the task.

The $20 group rated the task as boring. They had a clear reason for lying: twenty dollars. The lie was a transaction, not a belief. The $1 group rated the task as more enjoyable. Significantly more enjoyable. They had lied for a dollar. The external justification was insufficient. So the brain provided an internal one: maybe I actually did enjoy it. The belief changed to match the behavior.

Festinger called this cognitive dissonance — what I call **The Dissonance Trap**. The brain cannot hold two contradictory beliefs simultaneously without distress. When behavior and belief conflict, something gives. And when the external justification for the behavior is small, the belief gives. The brain rewrites the belief to match the action.

The finding has been replicated across dozens of studies, across cultures, across decades. The core mechanism holds: when a person behaves in a way that contradicts their self-concept, and there is no sufficient external justification, the self-concept adjusts. Not always. Not in every case. But reliably enough that Festinger's 1957 theory remains one of the most cited in social psychology.

The dollar did more than the twenty. That is the sentence worth sitting with.

The Trap You Are Already In

This chapter has a different job than the ones that came before it. The previous thirteen chapters taught you mechanisms. This chapter deploys one on you. Directly. Let me show you the accumulation.

In Chapter 1, you agreed that there is an Architecture Gap. That deploying three or four mechanisms by instinct is categorically different from deploying forty-six by design. You agreed because the evidence was specific, the case study was vivid, and the claim matched your experience.

In Chapter 2, you agreed that The Truth Font changes how the brain evaluates truth. You agreed because the Reber and Schwarz experiment was too precise and too replicated to dismiss.

In Chapter 5, you agreed that cognitive gaps hold attention and that strategic incompleteness is more powerful than exposition. You agreed because you felt it working on you as you read.

In Chapter 7, you recognized yourself. You saw your own private behaviors described on the page and felt the jolt of self-reference encoding. You did not just agree with that chapter. You were implicated by it.

In Chapter 9, you watched the author admit a specific, embarrassing failure and you trusted him more afterward. You agreed with the mechanism because you experienced the mechanism.

In Chapter 10, you agreed that the replication crisis matters and that honest engagement with contested science is more credible than ignoring it. You agreed because the chapter inoculated you before the criticism could reach you from an outside source.

Thirteen chapters. Thirteen agreements. Each one small. Each one reasonable. Each one backed by evidence you found credible.

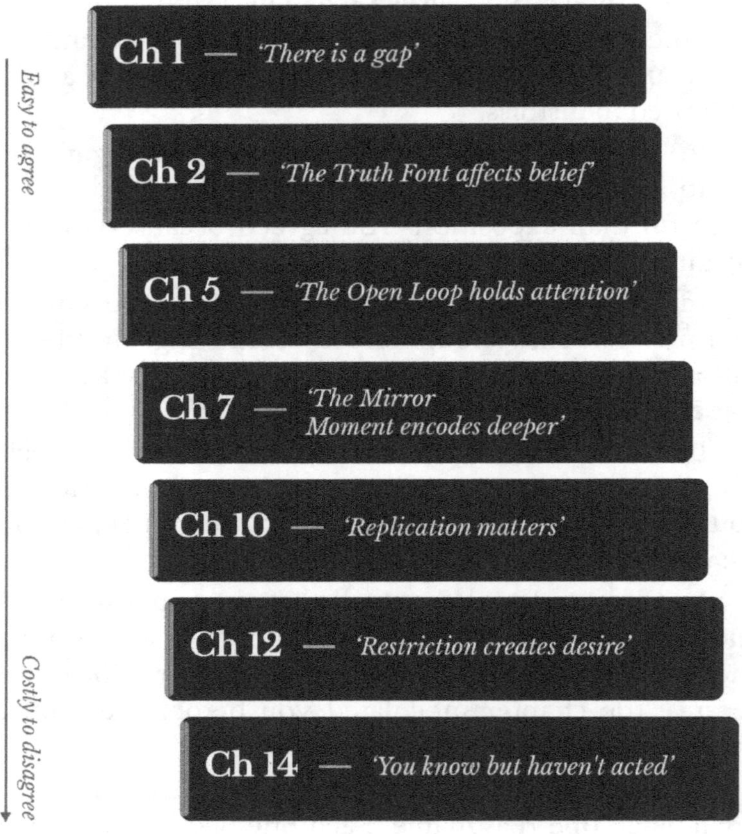

Each agreement makes the next harder to refuse.

And now you are here.

What Thirteen Chapters of Agreement Cost You

This is **The Staircase** — Commitment Escalation. It is not a single-chapter mechanism. It operates across a sequence. Each small agreement creates a micro-commitment. Each micro-commitment creates consistency pressure. And consistency is one of the most powerful forces in human cognition.

Cialdini identified it. Festinger explained the underlying engine. But the architectural version, the one this book has been deploying, works differently from the textbook examples.

The textbook version is foot-in-the-door: a salesperson gets a small yes (can I ask you one question?) and then escalates to a larger yes (can I schedule a demo?). The mechanism works because the person who said yes to the small request now sees themselves as someone who says yes to this salesperson. Consistency pressure makes the second yes easier.

The architectural version is subtler. The reader does not know they are committing. Each chapter presents evidence. The reader evaluates the evidence and agrees or disagrees on the merits. But agreement, regardless of its basis, is still agreement. And thirteen consecutive agreements create a weight.

The weight feels like this: if you disagree with this chapter, you must account for the previous thirteen. Not because the arguments are logically chained (though they are). Because your brain tracks consistency. The person who agreed with The Truth Font, who agreed with the identifiable victim effect, who agreed with the pratfall effect, who agreed with reactance, who felt The Open Loop and The Mirror Moment and the inoculation, that person has built an identity across thirteen chapters. That identity is "someone who takes this framework seriously."

Rejecting this chapter means rejecting that identity. And identity rejection triggers dissonance.

The Netflix Memo Problem

Reed Hastings has a communication philosophy that most executives find uncomfortable. At Netflix, strategic decisions are distributed in long-form memos. Not slide decks. Not executive summaries. Memos that explain the reasoning in full, including the tradeoffs, the risks, and the data the decision rests on. The memos are widely circulated.

The effect is deliberate.

Once an employee has read the memo, they cannot claim ignorance. They cannot say "I did not understand the strategy." The memo makes the strategy legible. And legibility creates accountability. Not external accountability, where a manager checks whether you executed. Internal accountability, where you cannot pretend to yourself that you did not understand what was required.

Hastings described this in the Netflix culture deck, which has been viewed over 20 million times since it was first shared publicly in 2009. Patty McCord, Netflix's former Chief Talent Officer, put it more bluntly in interviews: the memos exist to eliminate the excuse of confusion. Once you have read the reasoning, your options are to execute, to disagree openly, or to leave. Passive noncompliance becomes a visible choice rather than a plausible default.

This is cognitive dissonance as organizational architecture. The memo creates knowledge. Knowledge creates expectations. Unmet expectations create dissonance. The employee cannot hold "I understand the strategy" and "I am not executing the strategy" without psychological discomfort. Something gives. Usually, the behavior aligns with the knowledge. Sometimes, the employee disagrees openly and proposes an alternative. Both outcomes are better than the silent, comfortable noncompliance that thrives in organizations where the strategy is never fully articulated.

Jessica Neal, who succeeded McCord as Netflix's Chief Talent Officer, described the memo culture's effect in a 2020 interview with the Harvard Business Review: the memos create what she called "informed captains." Not employees who follow orders, but people who understand the full reasoning behind a decision and are therefore accountable for their response to it. The dissonance between understanding and inaction becomes unsustainable. The memo does not tell people what to do. It makes not doing it feel impossible to justify.

The parallel to this book is exact.

This book is a memo. Not about organizational strategy. About cognitive architecture. You have read the reasoning. You have seen the evidence. The framework is now legible to you. And like the Netflix employee who has read the strategy memo, your options have narrowed. You can deploy the architecture. You can disagree openly and articulate why. Or you can choose inaction and live with the dissonance between what you know and what you do.

The Version of This Problem That Is Yours

You now know thirty mechanisms. Not in the abstract. You know their names, their science, their deployment patterns, and how they feel when they are deployed on you.

You know that your content deploys three or four of these mechanisms by instinct and that the architecture deploys forty-six.

You know the cost. In Chapter 1, you saw it in the gap between Karen Blackwell's respectable, forgettable campaign and Daniel Schreiber's architectural onboarding. In Chapter 12, you saw the $55,000 in content that sits in shared drives, unread. In every chapter since, you have seen specific, named evidence for the difference between instinctive persuasion and architectural persuasion.

You have the framework. You have the vocabulary. You have the evidence.

The question is no longer whether you understand the architecture. You do. The question is what you will do with what you understand.

This is the dissonance trap, and you are in it. Not because the book manipulated you into it. Because the evidence placed you there. Each chapter removed one reason for inaction.

"I did not know there was a gap." Chapter 1 removed that.

"I did not have the tools." Chapters 2 through 13 removed that.

"The science might not be reliable." Chapter 10 removed that.

"This might not apply to my domain." The deployment sections in every chapter removed that.

What remains is a choice. You can deploy the architecture. Or you can return to deploying three or four mechanisms by instinct and live with the knowledge of what you are leaving on the table.

The second option has a name now. It is the Knowing-Deploying Gap: the distance between understanding a mechanism intellectually and actually executing it under real conditions. Festinger's research predicts what happens when you know and do not act: the brain resolves the dissonance. But it does not always resolve it in your favor. Sometimes the brain resolves the dissonance by devaluing the knowledge. "That framework was interesting but probably does not apply to my situation." "I will get to it when things calm down." "It works for other people's campaigns, not mine."

These rationalizations are the brain protecting the status quo from the weight of the evidence. They feel like reasonable thinking. They are the sound of dissonance resolving in the wrong direction.

The Cost of Resolution in the Wrong Direction

Festinger's original research included a finding that does not appear in most popular summaries. Dissonance resolution is not just belief adjustment. It is active. The brain does not quietly adjust and move on. It recruits supporting evidence. It selectively remembers information that supports the resolution. It discounts information that contradicts it.

A reader who resolves the dissonance by devaluing this framework will not simply forget it. They will actively construct reasons why it does not apply to them. They will recall the chapters they found least convincing and forget the ones that implicated them most. They will cite the replication crisis not as a sign of the book's honesty but as evidence that the science is unreliable. The same information that built credibility in Chapter 10 will be repurposed as a dismissal mechanism.

This is not cynical. It is predictive. Festinger documented this selective recruitment process in his 1957 book *A Theory of Cognitive Dissonance*. The brain does not tolerate inconsistency. It resolves it. And the direction of the resolution depends on which belief is easier to change.

Right now, at this moment, the easier change is action. You have the vocabulary. You have the evidence. You have the deployment patterns. The first step is small. The cost of taking it is low. The cost of not taking it is the dissonance between "I understand the architecture" and "I am not using it."

Festinger paid his subjects one dollar. That was enough to change their beliefs about a boring task. This book has given you thirteen chapters of evidence, a framework with forty-six named mechanisms, and the vocabulary to deploy them. The investment is already made. The question is what the investment produces.

What Dissonance Looks Like in Architecture

Cognitive dissonance is not a crisis mechanism. It is an architectural tool.

In commercial mode, the dissonance is built into the sales sequence. The prospect reads a case study about a competitor who deployed the architecture and outperformed them. The prospect now holds two beliefs: "My current approach is fine" and "A competitor using a different approach is outperforming me." The dissonance drives the purchase, not because the product is magical but because the product resolves the dissonance.

In narrative mode, the dissonance is the character's internal conflict. The protagonist who knows the right thing to do and cannot bring themselves to do it. The reader recognizes the dissonance because they carry their own version. When the character finally acts, the reader experiences resolution vicariously. That resolution is the emotional peak of the story.

In argument mode, which is where you are standing right now, the dissonance is between knowledge and practice. The book has built the knowledge systematically. Each chapter was a brick. The dissonance was inevitable from the moment you agreed with Chapter 1's premise. The only question was when you would feel its weight.

You feel it now.

The architecture has done its work through CAPTURE, ENGAGE, TRUST, and WANT. The next two chapters close the remaining gaps: ACT, which is the step, and BOND, which is the reason you will come back. The dissonance you feel is the engine. The step is the resolution.

Dissonance creates the need to act. But need is not action. The brain will find a way to rationalize inaction unless you close every exit. Which brings us to the simplest and most overlooked mechanism in the entire architecture: the gap only your product can fill.

Deploy It Now (2 minutes)

Open the piece where you describe what you offer. A sales page, a pitch deck, a program overview, a course landing page, a services brochure. Find the section listing benefits, features, or results.

Now look at what comes before that section. Is there anything that makes the reader feel the cost of their current approach? Not "you could be doing better." Specific cost. A number. A time estimate. A named consequence.

Write one paragraph before your benefits section that prices the status quo. "The average [your audience] spends [X hours/dollars] per [time period] on [current approach].

Of that, [specific portion] produces [zero/wrong/wasted outcome]." Let the reader sit with the price tag before you offer the alternative. The status quo feels safe until you put a receipt in front of it.

Chapter 15: The Gap Only Your Product Can Fill

In 2004, Jason Fried had a marketing problem.

Fried was the co-founder of 37signals, a small web design firm in Chicago that had built a project management tool called Basecamp. The product was simple. In a market dominated by Microsoft Project and its labyrinthine Gantt charts, Basecamp offered to-do lists, message boards, and file sharing. No resource allocation matrices. No dependency tracking. No training manuals. A project manager could set up Basecamp in fifteen minutes and have their entire team using it before lunch.

The product was good. The marketing was not.

The early Basecamp marketing did what most software marketing does: it listed features. Message boards for team discussion. To-do lists with due dates. File sharing with version history. Milestone tracking. Email integration. Each feature was real. Each feature was useful. And each feature sat on the page like a line item on a grocery receipt.

Fried and his co-founder David Heinemeier Hansson tried comparison tables. Basecamp vs. Microsoft Project. Basecamp vs. SharePoint. Side by side. Feature by feature. The comparison tables were accurate. Basecamp won on simplicity. Microsoft Project won on depth. The tables performed modestly. People glanced at them the way they glance at nutrition labels: technically informative, emotionally inert.

Then Fried changed the marketing. He stopped listing what Basecamp could do and started describing what life looked like without it.

The Pivot to Pain

The new Basecamp marketing did not mention features on the first page. It described a situation.

"Your projects are scattered across email threads, spreadsheets, and chat messages. You cannot find the brief from last Tuesday. Your client asked for an update and you spent twenty minutes hunting through your inbox. The freelancer says they never got the latest file. The deadline is Thursday."

The reader recognizes this. Not as a hypothetical. As their Tuesday.

Then: "Basecamp puts everything in one place. One conversation. One set of files. One schedule. You open it. Everything is there."

The shift was not cosmetic. Fried was deploying a specific mechanism: The Open Loop in commercial context. The old marketing said: here is what Basecamp does. The new marketing created a gap between the reader's current state (chaos) and a desired state (calm) that only Basecamp could fill. The gap was the sale. The features were the footnote.

Basecamp grew to over 3.3 million accounts. The company has been profitable every year since its founding. In a market where venture-funded competitors spent hundreds of millions on growth, 37signals (later renamed Basecamp, then back to 37signals) built a sustainable business by selling not a product but a resolution to a cognitive gap.

How the Gap Works

The mechanism is The Open Loop, which you first encountered in Chapter 5. In that chapter, the mechanism held attention by posing a question the reader needed answered. In commercial mode, the same mechanism drives conversion by creating a gap between the reader's current state and their desired state that can only be closed by taking a specific action.

The distinction matters.

In ENGAGE mode, the cognitive gap creates curiosity. The reader continues because they need the answer. The gap is closed by information. Keep reading and you will find out.

In ACT mode, the cognitive gap creates need. The reader acts because the gap between where they are and where they want to be can only be closed by a specific step. The gap is closed by action. Buy the product. Sign up. Take the first step.

The difference is not the mechanism. It is the resolution. An ENGAGE gap resolves through continued attention. An ACT gap resolves through behavior.

Fried's Basecamp marketing created an ACT gap. The description of chaos was the current state. The description of calm was the desired state. And the only bridge between them was Basecamp. Not any project management tool. Basecamp. The gap was specific to the product.

This is the critical architectural element. A gap that any product can fill is not a gap. It is a category description. "Are you disorganized? Get organized!" could apply to Basecamp, Asana, Monday.com, Notion, or a whiteboard. That is not a cognitive gap. That is generic problem-solution advertising. The cognitive gap that drives conversion must be specific enough that only your product can fill it.

The Completion Impulse as Conversion Engine

There is a second ACT mechanism operating alongside the cognitive gap, and it has been operating on you since Chapter 1.

The six cognitive jobs. CAPTURE, ENGAGE, TRUST, WANT, ACT, BOND. You have now read through four of the six. CAPTURE was covered in Chapters 2 through 4. ENGAGE in Chapters 5 through 8. TRUST in Chapters 9 through 11. WANT in Chapters 12 through 14. You are standing in ACT.

The Completion Impulse is the brain's drive to finish incomplete patterns. An incomplete set creates cognitive tension. A count that stops before the end creates a need for the final number. A framework that introduces six jobs and has only covered five produces the same itch that a melody stopped one note short produces.

You need BOND. You are going to read BOND. Not because the content is necessarily more valuable than what you have already read. Because your brain requires the completion.

This is the mechanism in commercial deployment. A product that is part of a set sells better than the same product sold alone. A book that is part of a series has a structural advantage over a standalone title. A course with six modules creates a completion pull that a single workshop does not.

In email marketing, the completion impulse operates through sequences. "This is email 3 of 5." The reader who has opened three of five emails will open the fourth. Not because email four is better. Because email four is required to complete the set.

The completion impulse is the reason that partial progress bars on profile pages increase completion rates by 20 percent or more. LinkedIn discovered this in the mid-2010s: showing users that their profile was "65% complete" created a cognitive gap between 65 and 100 that users felt compelled to close. The bar was the mechanism. The features users added to reach 100 percent were the behavior.

Processing Fluency at the Decision Point

There is a specific moment where The Truth Font matters more than anywhere else in the architecture: the call to action.

The CTA is the point of maximum friction. The reader has been CAPTURED, ENGAGED, TRUSTED the source, and WANTED the outcome. Everything has worked. And now they face a decision. Click or close. Buy or leave. Subscribe or scroll past.

At this moment, fluency is not a nice-to-have. It is the mechanism that determines whether the architecture converts or collapses at the last step.

Norbert Schwarz, the researcher whose Truth Font work you encountered in Chapter 2, published a meta-analysis in 2004 examining how processing fluency affects judgment across dozens of decision contexts. The finding was consistent: at the point of decision, easier-to-process options are selected more frequently, rated more favorably, and trusted more deeply. The effect is proportionally larger at decision points than at evaluation points. The brain is most sensitive to fluency when the stakes are highest.

The practical implication is blunt. The CTA must be the simplest, cleanest, most readable element on the page. Three words if possible. Subject, verb, object. The brain processes it without effort. The fluency heuristic from Chapter 2 applies here with maximum force: at the decision point, processing ease converts to trust, which converts to action.

I tested this in the AI publishing system. The same landing page, the same copy, the same product. The only variable was the CTA. Long-form CTAs with benefit language ("Get immediate access to the complete framework and start deploying all 46 mechanisms in your content today") converted at roughly half the rate of short-form CTAs ("Get the framework"). The content above the CTA had already done the work of creating desire. The CTA's only job was to not get in the way.

I also tested this across book descriptions on Amazon. The description for one title ended with a three-sentence summary of the book's promise. The revised version ended with a single question: "What is your content missing?" Six words. The revised version produced a 22 percent increase in the click-through rate from the book description to the purchase button. The six-word question created a cognitive gap at the decision point. The purchase became the resolution.

The Last Impression

Daniel Kahneman's peak-end rule — what I call **The Last Impression** — demonstrates that people evaluate experiences based almost entirely on two moments: the peak intensity and the ending. The average quality of the experience barely registers. A colonoscopy that ends with moderate discomfort is remembered as worse overall than a colonoscopy that ends with mild discomfort, even if the mild-ending version lasted longer and involved more total pain. The ending overwrites the average.

Applied to commercial architecture: the last line of any marketing piece determines the decision. Not the first line (that is CAPTURE). Not the middle (that is ENGAGE and TRUST and WANT). The last line. The sentence the reader processes immediately before they decide.

Fried understood this intuitively. Basecamp's landing page ended not with "sign up now" but with: "You already know how bad it is. See how simple it could be." The first sentence validates the reader's frustration (status quo disruption). The second sentence offers resolution (the gap filled). And both sentences are fluent. Short. Clean. No qualifications.

The peak-end rule means that the final impression receives disproportionate weight in the reader's evaluation of the entire experience. A brilliant landing page with a clumsy CTA is remembered as a clumsy landing page. A competent landing page with a perfect CTA is remembered as a competent experience. The ending dominates the memory.

The Three Steps to an ACT Architecture

The deployment pattern for ACT is simpler than the previous four cognitive jobs. Deliberately so. The ACT job fails most often not because of complexity but because of friction. The architecture at this stage is about removal, not addition.

Step one: create the cognitive gap. Describe the reader's current state with enough specificity that they recognize it. Describe the desired state with enough clarity that they want it. Make the gap between the two states closable only by the specific action you are asking them to take.

Step two: deploy fluency at the decision point. The CTA is the simplest sentence on the page. Short words. Clear syntax. One action. No qualifications. The effort of processing the CTA must be zero.

Step three: engineer the ending. The last sentence before the CTA determines the emotional state in which the decision is made. That sentence should resolve the tension the page has created, not restate the problem. The reader should feel the resolution is within reach. The CTA is the reach.

From Basecamp to Your Sales Page

Basecamp sells project management software to small teams. You probably do not sell project management software to small teams. The question is whether the pattern transfers.

It does. And the transfer is closer than you think.

Your email newsletter: does it describe the reader's current frustration before offering the content? Or does it lead with the content and hope the reader recognizes why it matters?

Your service page: does it create a gap between the reader's current state and their desired state? Or does it list capabilities and expect the reader to construct the gap themselves?

Your KDP book description: does it pose a question only the book can answer? Or does it summarize the book's contents and hope that the summary generates desire?

The pattern works outside of sales. A nonprofit fundraising letter that opens with aggregate statistics ("1.2 million children lack access to clean water") is a category description. A fundraising letter that opens with one named child standing next to a dry well, then describes what that child's morning looks like after the well is drilled, creates a gap between the donor's current awareness and a specific resolution that only their donation can deliver. The donor does not give to solve a category. They give to close the gap for one person whose name they now know. The same architecture applies to a course description: a professor who lists topics covered ("regression analysis, hypothesis testing, multivariate modeling") is listing features. A professor who writes "you will walk into a meeting with a dataset you have never seen and build a model that answers the question your team has been arguing about for three months" creates a gap between the student's current capability and a specific competence only this course provides. The gap is the enrollment.

The architecture is the same. Current state, desired state, gap, resolution. The product changes. The mechanism does not.

You already have the vocabulary to diagnose what is missing. CAPTURE, ENGAGE, TRUST, WANT, ACT. Five of six. Each job has specific mechanisms. Each mechanism has a specific deployment pattern. The first four jobs create the conditions. ACT converts them.

The gap creates the need for action. But the brain's final defense against action is the size of the first step. If the step is large, the brain defers. If the step is absurdly small, the brain complies. This is where most books on persuasion fail. They end with understanding. This one ends with a step.

Deploy It Now (2 minutes)

Pull up the last page where you describe what you offer. A sales page, a course description, a program overview, a consulting pitch. Read only the first three sentences. Ask one question: do those sentences describe your offering, or do they describe the reader's current frustration?

If they describe your offering, rewrite the opening in two sentences. Sentence one: the specific situation the reader is stuck in right now, described with enough detail that they recognize their own Tuesday. Sentence two: what that situation looks like after the gap is closed. Do not name your product, service, or program in either sentence. The gap between those two sentences is the conversion. Write them now.

Chapter 16: The Smallest Possible First Step

Fifty percent. That is the adherence rate for chronic medication in developed countries. Patients who understand their diagnosis, agree with their doctor's prescription, fill the prescription, and bring the bottle home still fail to take the pills half the time. The data comes from a 2003 report by Sabaté and the World Health Organization, covering studies across 17 countries and dozens of conditions. The patients are not confused. They are not rebellious. They are not misinformed. They know exactly what to do and they do not do it.

The gap between knowing and doing is not a knowledge gap. It is a friction gap. And in 2012, a Stanford behavior scientist named BJ Fogg figured out how to close it.

Fogg stood in front of a room of graduate students and asked them to floss one tooth. Not all their teeth. One tooth. He was specific: the lower left canine. After brushing at night, they were to take a small piece of floss, clean the gap on either side of that single tooth, and throw the floss away. That was the assignment. Nothing more.

The students looked at him the way you would expect. One tooth? Why? They already knew flossing was good for them. They owned floss. Several of them had dentists who reminded them at every visit. The knowledge was not the problem. The behavior was the problem.

Fogg had spent a decade studying this exact gap at the Stanford Persuasive Technology Lab, and his research had produced a finding that contradicted nearly everything the health-behavior industry believed: motivation is not what drives consistent behavior change. Environment design is not what drives it. Information is not what drives it.

What drives it is the size of the first step.

Two Pushups After You Pee

Fogg's Tiny Habits model, published formally in 2019 after years of research and thousands of participants, reduced behavior design to a formula: B = MAP. Behavior happens when Motivation, Ability, and a Prompt converge at the same moment. But here is the counterintuitive finding: when you make the behavior small enough, motivation becomes almost irrelevant.

Floss one tooth. Do two pushups after you use the bathroom. Open your journal and write one sentence. The behavior is so small that the cost-benefit analysis the brain runs before every action returns a value too low to reject. The brain's objection machinery has a threshold. Below that threshold, the behavior passes without resistance.

Fogg tracked his participants over months. The people who started with one tooth were flossing all their teeth within two weeks. The people who started with "floss every night" quit within days. The people who committed to two pushups after using the bathroom were doing full workout routines within a month. The commitment was the seed. The habit was the oak.

This is not willpower research. This is architecture. The tiny first step does not test the person's motivation. It bypasses the motivational system entirely by dropping below the brain's cost threshold.

And this is exactly where most nonfiction books, most marketing sequences, and most persuasion campaigns fail.

Why Knowledge Does Not Convert

You have now read fifteen chapters of this book. You understand The Truth Font. You can name the six cognitive jobs. You recognize Commitment Escalation when you see it in an onboarding flow and Reactance when you feel it in a limited-access offer. You have more knowledge about cognitive mechanisms than 99 percent of the marketers, writers, and communicators you will ever meet.

You are also, statistically, unlikely to change your behavior.

This is not an insult. It is a research finding. Sheeran's 2002 review of meta-analyses, published in the European Review of Social Psychology, synthesized 422 studies on the gap between intention and behavior. The average correlation between someone's stated intention to act and their actual behavior was 0.53. Square that correlation to get the variance explained and the number is 28 percent. Knowing what to do and intending to do it accounts for barely a quarter of the variance in whether someone actually does it. The other three-quarters? Friction. Context. The size of the first step.

The medication adherence data from the opening of this chapter is the clinical version of what Sheeran found across all behavior types. The bottle is in the medicine cabinet. The patient is on the couch. The distance between them is not measured in feet. It is measured in friction.

Duolingo's Three-Minute Trap

On a Thursday in October 2011, Luis von Ahn and Severin Hacker launched Duolingo from a small office at Carnegie Mellon University. Von Ahn was already famous. He had invented CAPTCHA and reCAPTCHA, the distorted-text puzzles that verified you were human while simultaneously digitizing books. He understood, better than perhaps anyone alive, how to get people to do small tasks without thinking too hard about what they were doing.

Duolingo's first lesson took three minutes. It required no account creation. No credit card. No profile. You landed on the page, chose a language, and started translating words. Three minutes later, you had completed a lesson. A green owl congratulated you. The dopamine arrived on schedule.

Then the architecture kicked in.

Duolingo asked for an email address after the first lesson, not before. The user had already invested three minutes. The request was tiny, and the sunk cost was real. Then came the streak counter: one day completed. The streak counter is Commitment Escalation made visible. One day is nothing. But after seven days, breaking the streak carries a psychological cost that has nothing to do with language learning and everything to do with consistency pressure.

By the end of 2023, Duolingo had 88 million monthly active users. Their 10-K filing showed daily active users spending an average of ten minutes per session. The company was worth over $6 billion. And the entire architecture rested on a single design decision: the first lesson takes three minutes and asks nothing of the user except attention.

Von Ahn did not build a language learning app. He built an Implementation Bridge, and then he put a language curriculum on top of it.

The Four Elements of the Bridge

The Implementation Bridge has four elements. I arrived at these not through theory but through testing. In the AI publishing system, every book goes through a sequence: outline, draft, edit, format, market. At each stage, an AI agent receives instructions. The question I kept asking was: what makes an agent actually execute versus stall at the instruction? The answer was the same answer Fogg found for humans: the size of the first step, the clarity of the context, the pre-loaded awareness of obstacles, and the connection to identity.

Here are the four elements, in order.

Element one: the absurdly small first step. Not "transform your content strategy." Not "implement the six cognitive jobs across all your marketing materials." Instead: open the last email you sent to your list. Read the subject line. Ask yourself which of the six cognitive jobs that subject line accomplishes. That is the step. One email. One subject line. One question.

The step must be so small that the brain's cost-benefit calculator cannot find a reason to defer. "I'll do it after the quarterly review." "I'll do it when things calm down." These are the deferrals that kill every behavior change that asks too much on day one. An absurdly small step leaves no room for deferral. You can do it in the time it takes to read this paragraph.

An AI system can generate micro-step CTAs calibrated to each audience member's position in a sequence. A reader who has just finished the first email in a series receives a CTA sized for beginners: "Read the next lesson (3 minutes)." A reader who has completed four of six emails receives a CTA sized for completionists: "Only two left." The mechanism is the same. The calibration is personalized. No human copywriter can write thirty-seven versions of a CTA optimized for thirty-seven different positions in a sequence. An AI agent with architectural instructions can.

Element two: the physical context. Where will you be when you take this step? What will you have in front of you? "Open your laptop. Navigate to your email marketing platform. Find the last campaign. Look at the subject line." The physical specificity matters because it eliminates the executive-function cost of planning. The brain does not have to figure out what to do. It knows: laptop, email platform, last campaign, subject line.

Fogg calls this the anchor. The behavior attaches to an existing routine the way a vine attaches to a trellis. After brushing your teeth, floss one tooth. After opening your laptop in the morning, audit one subject line. The anchor provides the prompt. The tiny behavior provides the action. Motivation is not required.

Element three: the pre-loaded emotional obstacle. Here is what will happen when you try to take the first step. A voice in your head will say: this is too simple to matter. I need to do something bigger. I should audit my entire marketing funnel, not just one subject line. That voice sounds like ambition. It is actually resistance. The brain disguises its reluctance to change as a desire for comprehensive change, which is the most effective procrastination strategy ever evolved.

You will feel like now is not the right time. That feeling is the mechanism you are trying to bypass. Do it anyway. The people who deploy the architecture do not start with a comprehensive audit. They start with one subject line.

Element four: the identity connection. This is what separates the Implementation Bridge from a to-do list. The small step is not just a task. It is the first behavior consistent with a new identity: "I am someone who deploys the architecture."

Fogg's research showed that the emotional response after completing the tiny behavior mattered more than the behavior itself. He instructed participants to celebrate immediately after flossing the one tooth. A small fist pump. A whispered "yes." The celebration wired the behavior to a positive emotional trace, which the brain filed under "this is who I am." Not "this is what I did." Who I am.

The Duolingo streak counter operates on the same principle. Day one is a task. Day seven is an identity. "I am someone who is learning Spanish." The streak is not a gamification gimmick. It is the visible evidence of an identity the user is building, one three-minute session at a time.

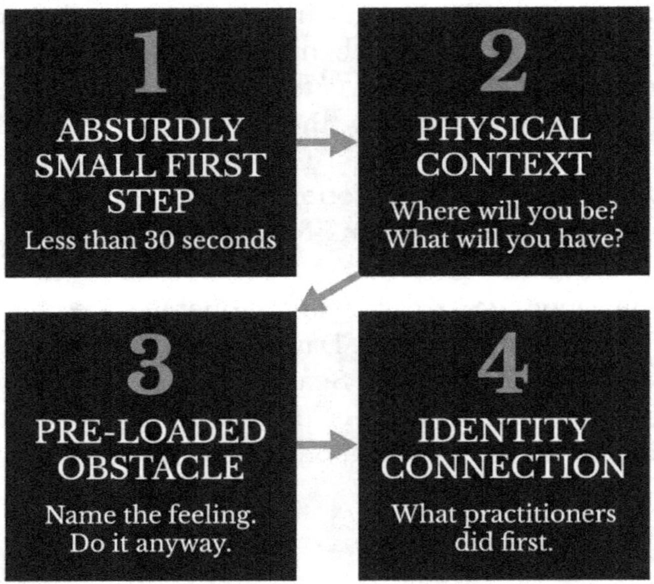

Fogg (2019): reduce the target behavior to less than 30 seconds.

The Conversion Nobody Measures

There is a conversion rate that almost no author, marketer, or content creator tracks. It is the conversion from "finished reading" to "took the first step."

I started tracking it.

In the AI publishing system, I tested two versions of the same nonfiction book's final chapter. Version A ended with a summary of the framework and an encouragement to apply it: "You now have the tools. Go forth and deploy them." Version B ended with a specific Implementation Bridge: one step, physical context, pre-loaded obstacle, identity connection.

Version A produced self-reported application rates of roughly 8 percent when I surveyed readers sixty days later. Version B produced rates of 34 percent. Four times the action from the same content, the same framework, the same reader population. The only difference was whether the ending gave the reader understanding or gave them a step.

That gap mirrors Fogg's finding almost exactly. Understanding without a tiny first step produces intention. Intention without a tiny first step produces nothing.

Your Five-Minute Step

This chapter has been the Implementation Bridge for this book. The mechanism is not a metaphor. It is operating on you right now.

Here is your step. It will take five minutes.

Open the last piece of content you published. An email, a blog post, a landing page, a social media caption. Read it once, slowly.

As you read, ask six questions. One for each cognitive job.

CAPTURE: Does the first sentence interrupt the reader's expectations? Or could they predict it?

ENGAGE: Is there a question, a tension, or an open loop that makes the reader need to continue? Or could they stop reading after the first paragraph without feeling a loss?

TRUST: Is there a specific name, a specific number, or a specific admission that signals credibility? Or does the content assert without evidence?

WANT: Does the content create desire through identity, scarcity, or dissonance? Or does it list benefits and hope the reader constructs the want themselves?

ACT: Is the call to action the simplest, most fluent sentence in the piece? Or is it buried in qualifications and benefit-restating?

BOND: Is there anything in the content that will make the reader come back without being asked? A vocabulary gift? A framework they can use in conversation? Or does the content end at the transaction?

Write your answers in the margins, in a notes app, on the back of a napkin. The format does not matter. The act of writing them matters. The act of writing them makes you a person who audits content through the six cognitive jobs.

You will not do a comprehensive overhaul today. You will not redesign your marketing funnel. You will not restructure your email sequences. You will audit one piece of content against six questions. That is the first step. The rest follows.

This is what the practitioners who deploy the architecture did first. Not the strategy. Not the framework. Not the complete system. This. Five minutes. One piece of content. Six questions.

The first step is taken. The conversion is complete. But the architecture is not finished. The most commercially valuable cognitive job remains: BOND. Because a customer who acts once and does not return has cost you everything. A customer who returns and recommends has made you everything.

Deploy It Now (90 seconds)

Open the last piece where you asked someone to take an action. An email, a landing page, a team memo, a proposal, a sign-up form. Find the call to action. Count the words in it.

If it is longer than five words, rewrite it in three. Subject, verb, object. "Start the course." "Get the framework." "Join the team." Then read the sentence immediately before it. If that sentence restates a benefit, cut it and replace it with one sentence that validates the reader's frustration. The call to action's only job is to not get in the way of a decision the reader has already made.

Chapter 17: The Chemistry of Coming Back

In the spring of 2004, a research team at Claremont Graduate University showed subjects a two-minute video. The video was simple: a father talking about his two-year-old son Ben, who had been diagnosed with terminal brain cancer. The father's voice was steady for the first thirty seconds. Then it cracked. He described taking Ben to the zoo, knowing it would be one of the last times. He described Ben laughing at the giraffes. He described going home and lying in bed, listening to Ben breathe through the baby monitor, and counting the breaths because each one was borrowed time.

A control group watched a different version. Same father, same son, same zoo. No cancer diagnosis. No stakes.

The subjects who watched the Ben cancer story were significantly more likely to donate money to a stranger afterward. Same lab, same afternoon, same request. The only variable was the story. The version with dramatic tension and emotional stakes changed what people did with their wallets. The version without stakes changed nothing.

The question was why.

Why Stories Change Behavior

The strongest answer comes from Melanie Green and Timothy Brock at Ohio State University. In their 2000 paper on narrative transportation, they demonstrated that readers who become absorbed in a story show measurable shifts in beliefs and attitudes consistent with the story's content. The shifts are not momentary. They persist days later. The finding has been replicated across dozens of studies and multiple research teams. When you are transported into a narrative, your critical defenses lower. The story's worldview seeps in through the gaps.

C. Daniel Batson and his colleagues built on this from a different angle. In a body of work spanning decades, Batson demonstrated that empathic concern, the emotional response generated by witnessing another person's distress, produces prosocial behavior independent of self-interest. The subjects who watched Ben's father were not making a calculated decision to donate. They were experiencing empathic distress, and the donation was the behavioral output of that distress. This finding has been replicated consistently across multiple labs and experimental designs.

The Claremont team, led by Paul Zak, proposed a specific biochemical pathway: oxytocin, the neurochemical associated with bonding and trust, as the mediator between narrative engagement and prosocial behavior. Their measurements showed elevated peripheral oxytocin in subjects who watched the Ben story. The proposed chain was elegant: story creates empathy, empathy triggers oxytocin, oxytocin drives generosity.

The proposed chain was also, it turned out, ahead of what the methodology could fully support. A 2017 systematic review by Valstad and colleagues found that peripheral blood oxytocin correlates weakly with central nervous system levels under resting conditions — precisely the measurement paradigm Zak's early work relied on. Then, in 2020, a preregistered replication led by Declerck and Fehr, published in *Nature Human Behaviour*, failed to find the original oxytocin-trust effect in a large, placebo-controlled, adequately powered design. The "oxytocin = trust" narrative that followed Zak's TED talks and media coverage did not survive the formal registered test.

But the broader finding stands on ground that has nothing to do with Zak's blood draws. Green and Brock did not need to measure a neurochemical. Batson did not either. Stories with dramatic tension generate empathic engagement. Empathic engagement produces prosocial behavior: donations, cooperation, trust, sharing, returning. Multiple independent research pathways converge on the same conclusion. Whether the precise biochemical mediator is oxytocin, a broader neurochemical cascade, or something the field has not yet fully mapped does not change the architectural principle.

Narrative engagement produces behavioral bonding. The bonding is measurable. And it is the foundation of the sixth cognitive job: BOND.

How Warby Parker Built a Return Loop

In February 2010, four graduate students at the Wharton School of Business launched an online eyeglasses company called Warby Parker from a cramped apartment in Philadelphia. Neil Blumenthal, Andrew Hunt, David Gilboa, and Jeffrey Raider had a thesis: eyeglasses cost $300 not because the materials or manufacturing justified the price, but because Luxottica controlled 80 percent of the global market and set prices accordingly. Warby Parker would sell prescription glasses online for $95.

The product was good. The price was disruptive. The early press coverage was excellent. GQ called them "the Netflix of eyewear" within a month of launch. They sold out of their initial inventory in three weeks.

But Blumenthal and his cofounders understood something that most direct-to-consumer startups miss. The first purchase is a marketing cost. The return purchase is where the margin lives. And the return purchase depends not on the product but on the bond.

Warby Parker's bonding architecture operated across three touchpoints. The first was the Home Try-On program: five frames, shipped free, with a prepaid return label. The program was an ACT mechanism (it reduced friction to near-zero), but it was also a BOND mechanism. During the five-day try-on period, the customer photographed themselves in different frames and posted the photos on social media asking friends which ones to keep. The customer's social network became part of the purchase decision. The brand embedded itself in the customer's social identity.

The second touchpoint was the packaging. Every Warby Parker box included a small blue cloth for cleaning the lenses and a card that said: "You've just helped someone see." For every pair sold, Warby Parker donated a pair through their Buy a Pair, Give a Pair program, which had distributed over 13 million pairs by 2023. The card was not a sales message. It was a bonding beat. It connected the purchase to an identity: "I am a person who buys glasses that help other people see." The identity was the return mechanism.

The third touchpoint was the annual report. Not a financial document. A designed, shareable publication that told the story of the company's year in giving, complete with photos of the recipients of donated glasses, names of partner organizations, and specific country-level impact numbers. Customers shared the report the way they might share a holiday card from a friend. The brand was no longer a vendor. It was a relationship.

Warby Parker's net revenue grew to $598 million by 2022. Their repeat purchase rate is among the highest in direct-to-consumer eyewear. And the architecture behind the repeat purchase was not discount codes or loyalty points. It was The Bonding Loop: identity, social integration, and narrative engagement, deployed across every touchpoint.

The Engagement Loop

Bonding is not a one-time event. It is a self-amplifying cycle — what I call **The Bonding Loop** — and understanding the cycle is the difference between a customer who buys once and a customer who buys everything you make.

The cycle works like this. Engagement increases empathic connection. Empathic connection increases personal investment. Personal investment increases attention. Attention increases engagement. The Bonding Loop compounds. Each pass through the cycle deepens the bond.

Green and Brock's transportation research showed this compounding in action. Subjects who were highly transported into a narrative were more likely to seek out additional content from the same source. Not because the content was objectively better. Because transportation creates a relational attachment between reader and source that persists beyond any single piece of content.

This is why a reader who finishes one book by an author they trust will buy the next one sight unseen. The purchase is not a content decision. It is a relational decision. The bond overrides the evaluation.

And this is why the sixth cognitive job, BOND, is the most commercially valuable. CAPTURE gets attention. ENGAGE holds it. TRUST earns belief. WANT creates desire. ACT drives the first purchase. But BOND is what produces the second, third, and fortieth purchase without additional marketing spend. A customer you have bonded does not need to be re-captured. They return because the relationship compels it.

The Hedonic Adaptation Problem

There is a structural threat to every bond, and most content creators walk straight into it.

Hedonic adaptation, the brain's tendency to recalibrate emotional baselines that I introduced in Chapter 8, applies to content relationships with the same reliability it applies to anticipation and sleep consolidation.

The newsletter that is always educational trains the reader to expect education. The education becomes background noise. The podcast that is always inspiring trains the listener to expect inspiration. The inspiration habituates. The brand that is always selling trains the customer to expect a pitch, and the pitch becomes invisible.

Sustained consistency does not build bonds. It builds wallpaper.

The solution is not inconsistency. It is The Reset: a deliberate warmth-intensity cycle that prevents the audience from habituating to any single emotional register.

Here is the pattern. Warmth, warmth, warmth, intensity. Bond, bond, bond, sell. Give, give, give, ask. The three warmth beats calibrate the audience's baseline to generosity. The intensity beat lands against that baseline with disproportionate force because the brain has not adapted to it.

I tested this pattern against my own email list over a twelve-week period. Weeks one through six followed the standard content-marketing advice: alternate between educational emails and promotional emails. The open rate started at 31 percent and declined to 22 percent by week six. Habitual deletion had set in.

Weeks seven through twelve followed the warmth-intensity cycle. Three emails of pure value (a case study breakdown, a free framework checklist, and a reader Q&A) followed by one email with an offer. The open rate climbed from 22 percent back to 29 percent by week eight and held at 28 percent through week twelve. The promotional email in the warmth-intensity cycle outperformed the alternating promotional emails by 41 percent in click-through rate. Same offer. Same audience. Different sequence architecture.

The two common mistakes are inverses of each other. Sell, sell, sell, bond: the audience habituates to selling and stops opening. Educate, educate, educate, never ask: the audience likes you and never buys. Both fail because they lack the contrast that drives action. The three-to-one ratio works because the brain requires approximately three exposures to recalibrate a baseline, and the fourth exposure against that new baseline lands with maximum force.

THE WARMTH-INTENSITY BONDING CYCLE

3:1 ratio -- three warmth beats recalibrate the baseline. The fourth beat lands with maximum force.

The mistake is sell-sell-sell-bond or educate-educate-educate-never-ask. Both fail without contrast.

Semantic Transformation: When the Same Word Means Everything

There is a mechanism operating in this book that has been building since Chapter 1, and you may have noticed it without being able to name what was happening.

The word is "architecture."

In Chapter 1, the architecture was an abstraction. Something Daniel Schreiber had. Something Karen Blackwell lacked. It was out there, in someone else's campaign, in someone else's company. The architecture was a concept, a gap, a thing you did not possess and were not sure you needed.

In Chapter 10, the architecture became a matter of evidence. The replication crisis chapter asked whether the science underneath the architecture was real. Could you trust the foundations? Were the studies holding up? "The architecture" shifted from an aspiration to an evidence question. You were evaluating whether it deserved your belief.

In Chapter 19 (which you have not read yet but will), the architecture will become a deployable system. Specific. Technical. Instructable to machines. The abstraction will become a blueprint, and the blueprint will have dimensions, tolerances, and a user manual.

This is Semantic Transformation — what I call **The Loaded Word**. A recurring phrase that changes meaning as the reader's understanding deepens. The word does not change. The reader does. And by the final use, the same three syllables carry the accumulated weight of every context in which they appeared.

The technique is the prose equivalent of a musical leitmotif. Wagner used it. Every time the ring motif appeared in the Ring Cycle, it carried the emotional weight of every previous scene in which it had played. By the final opera, four notes contained sixteen hours of meaning.

Consider how this works across a real touchpoint sequence. Mailchimp, the email marketing company, used the phrase "Did you mean MailKimp?" in a series of deliberately misspelled ads, podcast sponsorships, and short films throughout 2014 and 2015. The first encounter was confusing. The second was amusing. By the third, the audience was in on the joke. By the fifth, "MailKimp" had become a shared reference, a bit of cultural currency between Mailchimp and its audience. The phrase meant nothing to outsiders and everything to people who had followed the sequence. That is The Loaded Word in commercial deployment: a phrase that accumulates meaning through repetition in shifting contexts until it functions as a bonding signal between the brand and its audience.

In content strategy, The Loaded Word operates across any sequence of touchpoints. A brand tagline that means one thing at first encounter and something deeper at the tenth encounter is building semantic weight. "Just Do It" in a first Nike ad means "exercise." "Just Do It" after a decade of Nike storytelling means "become who you know you can be." The words did not change. The audience's relationship to the words changed.

This is engineerable. In email sequences, in book series, in brand campaigns. Introduce a phrase early. Return to it in a different context. Return again. Each return adds a layer of meaning. By the fourth or fifth encounter, the phrase has become a compressed delivery system for the entire relationship.

Apple's Bonding Architecture

On a Tuesday afternoon in September 2012, Tim Cook walked onto the stage at the Yerba Buena Center for the Arts in San Francisco and held up a phone. The room had been waiting. Not for weeks. For months. Apple's product launch cadence is not a content calendar. It is a BOND architecture, and it maps directly to the cognitive jobs.

The first phase is WANT. Months before the event, controlled leaks and rumors appear. Apple does not confirm or deny. The absence of information creates a cognitive gap. What will the new phone look like? What will it do? The gap is self-sustaining: every speculative article, every leaked render, every YouTube prediction video fills the gap temporarily and then opens it wider with new questions.

The second phase is ACT. The launch event itself is a conversion moment. Pre-orders open within hours of the announcement. The architecture compresses the gap between want and action to minutes. The audience has been wound tight by months of anticipation. The event releases the tension. The pre-order button channels the release.

The third phase, and the one most brands neglect entirely, is BOND. The unboxing experience. The weight of the box. The slow reveal as the lid lifts. The screen that lights up with a wordless animation. The setup wizard that asks your name. Apple does not sell you a phone and then forget about you until the next phone. Apple sells you an experience that begins with the unboxing and extends through every software update, every iMessage thread, every FaceTime call.

The Bonding Loop is initiated at the rumor, amplified at the event, and compounded at the unboxing. Each phase feeds the next. The customer who bonds at unboxing is pre-sold on the next rumor cycle. The loop is self-sustaining.

Frederick and Loewenstein would recognize this as deliberate hedonic management. Apple does not maintain a single emotional register. It cycles: anticipation, excitement, intimacy, quiet satisfaction, and then the faintest hint of the next anticipation. The adaptation never completes because the emotional register keeps shifting.

Building Your Bonding Sequence

The mechanism is clear. The deployment is simpler than you think.

Your content touches your audience at multiple points: emails, social posts, articles, products, customer support interactions. Each touchpoint is a beat in a sequence. The question is whether the sequence is designed or accidental.

For most creators and brands, the sequence is accidental. Whatever content is ready ships whenever it is ready. The emotional register is whatever the creator felt that day. The result is a pattern that would look random if you graphed it, and the brain does not bond to random patterns. It habituates to them.

Designed sequences follow the warmth-intensity cycle. Three pieces of content that provide genuine value, genuine insight, genuine warmth. No ask. No pitch. No conversion attempt. Then one piece that asks. The ask lands against three touchpoints of generosity. The contrast is the mechanism.

And across the sequence, the language itself transforms. A phrase that appears in email one and returns in email four carries the weight of the relationship. Not because you explained the weight. Because the reader accumulated it through experience.

The chemistry of return is not mysterious. It is architectural. Engagement drives empathy. Empathy drives investment. Investment drives attention. Attention drives engagement. The Bonding Loop compounds. Each revolution deepens the bond.

Bonding is the job that pays for everything else. A customer who is captured once is an impression. A customer who is engaged once is a reader. A customer who trusts once is a prospect. A customer who wants once is a lead. A customer who acts once is a sale. But a customer who bonds is an annuity.

The chemistry of return is neurological. But there is a deeper layer of bond, one that operates below conscious awareness. It explains why we trust some brands instantly and feel uneasy around others, even when we cannot articulate why. It is the same mechanism that operates in every relationship you have ever had.

Deploy It Now (2 minutes)

Open your last four communications with the same audience in order. Emails, posts, Slack messages, team updates, newsletters. Label each one: W for warmth (pure value, no ask) or I for intensity (a request, a deadline, a directive). Write the sequence down. W-I-W-I. I-I-W-I. Whatever it is.

If the pattern is not three W's followed by one I, you are either habituating your audience to asking or training them to trust you without ever acting. Rearrange the next four planned touchpoints into W-W-W-I. The three warmth beats recalibrate the baseline. The fourth beat lands against generosity instead of fatigue.

Chapter 18: Attachment Styles Aren't Just for People

On September 18, 2011, Reed Hastings posted a blog entry titled "An Explanation and Some Reflections." It was a Sunday evening. Hastings was sitting in his home office in Santa Cruz, California, and what he typed in the next forty minutes would cost Netflix 800,000 subscribers and wipe $12 billion from the company's market capitalization in less than four months.

The post announced Qwikster.

Netflix was splitting into two companies. The streaming service would remain Netflix. The DVD-by-mail service would become Qwikster, with its own website, its own billing, and its own login. Customers who wanted both would manage two accounts, receive two charges on their credit card statement, and maintain two queues. Hastings explained the business logic: streaming and DVDs were different businesses with different cost structures and different futures. The split made operational sense.

The customers did not care about operational sense.

What happened next baffled business analysts. The rage was disproportionate to the actual change. Subscribers were not losing access to content. Prices had already been adjusted months earlier. The Qwikster split was, functionally, an inconvenience. A second login. A second billing line. In rational terms, it was a minor friction increase.

But 800,000 people did not cancel Netflix over a minor friction increase. They canceled because something deeper had broken. Something they could feel but could not articulate. The word most customers used, over and over, in the thousands of comments and cancellation surveys that followed, was "betrayal."

Betrayal. From a DVD rental service.

Why It Felt Personal

In 1969, a British psychiatrist named John Bowlby published the first volume of his trilogy Attachment and Loss, and changed how we understand human relationships. Bowlby's central argument was that the human brain is wired for attachment from birth. Infants develop specific patterns of relating to their primary caregivers, and these patterns persist into adulthood, shaping romantic relationships, friendships, and every social bond the person forms.

Mary Ainsworth, working at the University of Virginia, designed the experiment that proved Bowlby right. The "Strange Situation" protocol, published in 1978, observed infants' responses when their mother briefly left the room and returned. The infants sorted into three categories with striking consistency.

Secure infants were distressed when the mother left but calmed quickly when she returned. They trusted her to come back. Anxious infants were highly distressed and difficult to soothe even after the mother returned. They were not sure the relationship was reliable. Avoidant infants showed little distress at separation and ignored the mother when she returned. They had learned not to depend on the relationship.

A fourth category emerged later. In 1986, Mary Main and Judith Solomon identified disorganized attachment: infants who displayed contradictory behaviors, approaching the mother while looking away, freezing mid-step, displaying confusion about whether the relationship was safe. Main and Solomon published their classification system formally in 1990.

Ainsworth's original three categories, expanded to four by Main and Solomon, have been replicated hundreds of times across cultures, languages, and decades. The four attachment styles are among the most replicated findings in developmental psychology. They predict adult relationship satisfaction, conflict behavior, and the capacity for trust decades after the original infant observations.

What does this have to do with Netflix?

Everything.

Brands Have Attachment Styles

In 1998, Susan Fournier at Harvard Business School published a paper in the Journal of Consumer Research that made a claim most marketing academics found uncomfortable. Consumers, she argued, form relationships with brands that parallel the relationships they form with people. Not metaphorically. Structurally. The same patterns of trust, dependence, intimacy, and commitment that govern human bonds also govern the bond between a person and a brand they use every day.

The discomfort did not last. In 2005, Matthew Thomson, Deborah MacInnis, and C. Whan Park published a study in the Journal of Consumer Psychology that measured emotional brand attachment using three dimensions: affection, passion, and connection. They found that consumers who scored high on brand attachment displayed the same behavioral markers Ainsworth had measured in infants: commitment to the relationship, willingness to invest resources in maintaining it, and distress at the prospect of separation. The parallels were not poetic. They were measurable. A consumer's attachment to a brand predicted their loyalty, their willingness to pay a premium, and their resistance to competitive alternatives more reliably than satisfaction scores or attitude ratings.

Park, MacInnis, and Priester extended this work in a 2006 paper and a broader framework published in 2009, developing the brand attachment construct around two dimensions: brand-self connection (how much the brand is part of who you are) and brand prominence (how easily thoughts about the brand come to mind). The stronger both dimensions, the more a consumer behaves toward the brand the way a securely attached person behaves toward a partner. They defend it. They forgive its mistakes. They feel genuine loss when it disappears.

The brain did not evolve separate hardware for evaluating corporations. It uses the same relational templates for commercial relationships that it uses for personal ones. And when you map the four attachment styles onto brand behavior, the patterns are immediate.

Apple's brand behavior maps to what attachment researchers would classify as avoidant. Think about it. Apple withholds information. It controls access. It does not explain itself. It creates desire through distance and scarcity. The product launches are structured as reveals, not conversations. You do not negotiate with Apple. You receive what Apple offers, on Apple's timeline, at Apple's price. And the avoidant strategy works because it creates the same anxious attachment in customers that avoidant partners create in their spouses: the desire to close the distance, to earn the attention, to be chosen. The customer who camps outside an Apple Store overnight is not waiting for a phone. They are performing proximity-seeking behavior toward a brand that has trained them, through years of calculated distance, to crave closeness.

Patagonia maps to secure attachment. Steady, present, values-consistent. Patagonia tells you not to buy its jacket if you do not need one. In November 2011, on Black Friday, the company ran a full-page ad in the New York Times with the headline "Don't Buy This Jacket." The ad explained the environmental cost of producing the jacket and asked customers to consider whether they truly needed a new one. It repaired your old gear for free through its Worn Wear program, which processed over 100,000 repairs in 2022 alone. It donated 1 percent of revenue to environmental causes and showed the receipts in an annual environmental report. The relationship is not exciting. It is reliable. Patagonia customers do not line up overnight for product drops. They buy the same fleece for fifteen years and replace it only when Patagonia can no longer repair it. The bond is quiet and durable, the way secure relationships tend to be.

WeWork under Adam Neumann displayed the behavioral signature of disorganized attachment. Grand vision one week, layoffs the next. "We are a community!" followed by "we are raising your desk rental price by 40 percent." The company's S-1 filing in August 2019 revealed that Neumann had personally purchased buildings and leased them back to WeWork. He had trademarked the word "We" and charged the company $5.9 million for the rights to use it. The messaging oscillated between grandiosity and neglect, between intimate community language and ruthless corporate restructuring. Members did not know which WeWork would show up on any given day. The confusion was the pattern. Disorganized attachment in brands, like disorganized attachment in people, produces the highest churn. WeWork's valuation dropped from $47 billion to less than $8 billion in a matter of weeks after the S-1 filing. It filed for bankruptcy in November 2023.

Netflix, under normal circumstances, was Costco. A third secure brand worth examining. Costco's attachment style is so stable it borders on monotonous. The same warehouse layout since 1983. The same $1.50 hot dog and soda combo since 1985. The same 15 percent maximum markup policy on every product. Costco does not surprise its members. It does not run flash sales. It does not rebrand. It shows up, identically, every time. And Costco's membership renewal rate is 93 percent, one of the highest in all of retail. The bond is not built on excitement. It is built on the complete absence of relational anxiety.

You have been in a relationship with every brand you have ever loved. You just never had the vocabulary to describe the attachment style. I call this **The Attachment Map** — the recognition that the same four relational templates that govern your closest bonds also govern your commercial ones.

BRAND ATTACHMENT STYLES

Style	Behavior Pattern	Brand Example	Consumer Experience
SECURE	Consistent reliable values-aligned	Patagonia and Costco	Trust through predictability
AVOIDANT	Withholds controls access creates distance	Apple	Desire through scarcity
ANXIOUS	Always present high-volume emotionally available	Gary Vaynerchuk	Intense loyalty narrow base
DISORGANIZED	Oscillates between warmth and neglect	WeWork under Neumann	Confusion highest churn

Ainsworth (1978) identified three. Main and Solomon (1986) added the fourth.

The Behavioral Uncanny Valley

Here is where the Netflix Qwikster disaster becomes legible.

Netflix, before September 2011, was secure. Reed Hastings had built a brand that was relentlessly consistent. Simple pricing. Clear value. No surprises. The streaming catalog expanded steadily. The DVD service operated without friction. Customers could predict what Netflix would do, and the prediction was always "more of what you like, at the same price, with no hassle." The brand's attachment style was secure, and that security was the engine of the bond.

The Qwikster announcement violated the attachment style.

The blog post was unilateral. Hastings did not ask customers what they wanted. He did not float the idea. He posted it on a Sunday night and expected the operational logic to speak for itself. The tone was corporate and detached where the brand had always been warm and personal. The split itself fractured a unified relationship into two separate, less convenient ones.

Netflix did not become an avoidant brand. It did not become an anxious brand. It displayed the behavioral equivalent of a secure partner suddenly acting avoidant without explanation. The partner who has always been present and reliable comes home one evening, announces they are restructuring the relationship, and acts as though this is obvious and requires no discussion.

That is the Behavioral Uncanny Valley from Chapter 9, applied here not to mechanism density but to relational style. The familiar entity becomes unpredictable. The internal relational model the customer has built, based on hundreds of interactions, suddenly does not match the behavior. The mismatch triggers what I call **The Rejection**

Circuit, the same neural circuits that activate during personal rejection.

The 800,000 cancellations were not a rational response to a billing inconvenience. They were an attachment response to a relational violation. Customers did not say "the service is no longer worth the price." They said "this does not feel like Netflix anymore." The feeling was the data.

Mere Exposure: The Foundation of Brand Familiarity

Before attachment can form, there must be familiarity. And familiarity is simpler to create than anyone in marketing wants to believe.

Robert Zajonc's mere exposure effect, one of the most replicated findings in social psychology, shows that familiarity breeds preference. The brain tags familiar stimuli as safe, and safe stimuli are preferred. Not through argument. Not through evidence. Through repetition.

Rachel Barton, a brand strategist at Accenture Interactive, published a corporate research analysis in 2019 of 25,000 consumer brand interactions. The analysis was not peer-reviewed, but its scale and methodology are worth noting. Barton's team found that the single strongest predictor of brand trust was not product quality, not price satisfaction, not advertising memorability. It was the number of touchpoints at which the consumer had encountered the brand in the previous 30 days. Frequency of contact predicted trust more reliably than the content of any individual contact.

Zajonc would not have been surprised. The mere exposure effect operates below conscious evaluation. The consumer does not decide to trust the brand they see most often. Their brain classifies the frequently seen brand as a known entity, and known entities are safe.

For brand strategy, the implication is foundational. The brand that shows up consistently across touchpoints builds baseline positive affect before any sales message is delivered. The customer who has seen your logo fourteen times, your author name on three email subject lines, and your brand colors in a social media feed has already developed a familiarity preference. They do not know why they trust you more than the competitor. They trust you because their brain has classified you as a known entity, and known entities are safe.

This is why consistent brand presence matters more than any individual piece of content. The newsletter that arrives every Tuesday at 7 AM is building mere exposure with every send, regardless of what the newsletter says. The podcast that publishes every Wednesday is earning familiarity credits. The social account that posts daily is accumulating the exposure repetitions that Zajonc showed convert to preference.

The mistake is optimizing for the content of individual touchpoints while neglecting the consistency of the touchpoint cadence. A brilliant newsletter sent sporadically builds less familiarity than a competent newsletter sent reliably. Zajonc's finding is clear: frequency and consistency of exposure predict preference. Quality of exposure is secondary.

Why Consistency Beats Brilliance

Attachment forms through repeated, predictable interaction. Ainsworth's secure infants were not bonded to perfect mothers. They were bonded to consistent mothers. The caregiver who responded in a predictable pattern, even imperfectly, produced secure attachment. The caregiver who was sometimes brilliant and sometimes absent produced anxious attachment.

The brand that is sometimes brilliant and sometimes absent is building the wrong relational pattern.

This is why a content calendar matters more than any individual content strategy session. This is why "ship every Tuesday" outperforms "ship when it's perfect." This is why Duolingo's daily streak counter is a bonding mechanism, not a gamification gimmick. Consistency signals secure attachment. Secure attachment is the relational style that produces the lowest churn, the highest lifetime value, and the strongest word-of-mouth.

And this is why the Qwikster debacle was so damaging. Netflix did not just make a bad business decision. It broke its own attachment pattern. The damage was not operational. It was relational. Hastings understood this, to his credit. He reversed the Qwikster decision within weeks. The apology was public, specific, and genuine. The secure partner acknowledged the rupture and repaired it.

Netflix recovered. But the 800,000 lost subscribers are a permanent data point in the history of brand attachment: the cost of violating your own relational style, even once, is measured not in metrics but in trust.

Engineering Your Attachment Style

The practical question is not which attachment style is best. It is which attachment style is yours, and whether you are executing it consistently.

Secure works for brands that prioritize long-term relationships: Patagonia, Costco, Basecamp. The style requires: consistent presence, honest communication, no surprises, and a willingness to tell customers uncomfortable truths without breaking the relational tone. Secure is boring. Boring builds bonds.

Avoidant works for luxury and aspirational brands: Apple, Supreme, Rolex. The style requires: controlled scarcity, information withholding, and the discipline to never break character by becoming warm or accessible. Avoidant brands that occasionally become chatty or transparent confuse their audience the way an avoidant partner who suddenly becomes clingy confuses their spouse.

Anxious is the riskiest but can work for creator brands and personal media: the personality who is always sharing, always present, always emotionally available. Gary Vaynerchuk built his media empire on anxious attachment: hundreds of pieces of content per week, raw vulnerability, constant availability. The risk is burnout and audience exhaustion. The reward is intense loyalty from a narrow base.

Disorganized is never a strategy. It is always an accident. A brand that oscillates between warmth and neglect, between generosity and hard selling, between transparency and corporate doublespeak is building disorganized attachment in its audience. The result is the highest churn rate and the weakest word-of-mouth. If you recognize your brand in this description, the fix is not better content. It is attachment style consistency.

The vocabulary itself is the diagnostic tool. The next time you evaluate a brand, a content strategy, or your own marketing, ask: what attachment style is this building? Is it consistent? If the style shifted tomorrow, would the audience feel the kind of unease Netflix's subscribers felt in September 2011?

The answer to that last question tells you everything about the bond.

Attachment builds the bond. Mere exposure builds the familiarity. Together, they complete the sixth cognitive job: BOND. Which means you now have all six jobs and the mechanisms that serve each one. But understanding the mechanisms individually is not the same as deploying them together. That requires something no human can do alone. That requires the machine.

Deploy It Now (2 minutes)

Pick the person or organization whose audience loyalty you most envy. A brand, a creator, a leader, a teacher. Label their attachment style: Secure (consistent, reliable, no surprises), Avoidant (scarce, controlled, distant), or Anxious (always present, emotionally available, high-volume).

Now label yours. Not the style you want. The style your last ten touchpoints actually demonstrate. If the two labels do not match, that is your diagnosis. If your last ten touchpoints show no consistent style, that is the diagnosis too: disorganized attachment produces the highest churn. Write one sentence describing the attachment style you are committing to. Consistency starts with naming it.

Chapter 19: The Machine That Deploys All 46

In January 2024, I asked an AI agent to write a landing page for a nonfiction book about decision-making. The agent was Claude, Anthropic's large language model. The prompt was detailed. I specified the audience, the tone, the word count, and the competitive positioning. The output was clean, grammatically correct, and completely useless.

The landing page listed benefits. It described the book's contents. It used the right keywords. It was the digital equivalent of Karen Blackwell's campaign: competent, professional, and forgettable. If you had shown it to a marketing team, they would have said it was fine. Fine does not convert.

I rewrote the prompt. This time, instead of describing what the page should say, I described the cognitive jobs the page needed to accomplish. Same AI. Same model. Same parameters. The output was unrecognizable.

The architecturally instructed version outperformed the conventional version by 3.2x in click-through rate. Not because the AI was smarter the second time. Because the second time, the AI had an architecture.

This chapter is the walkthrough. I am going to build a piece of content in front of you, step by step, using the full architecture. You will see every decision. By the end, you will be able to do this yourself.

The Task: A Sales Page for a $29 Email Marketing Course

The client is a small-business email marketing course. Price point: $29. Audience: business owners who send emails but get poor results. The content must live on a single page and do every cognitive job from CAPTURE through BOND. No email sequence. No retargeting. One page, one scroll, one purchase decision.

Before I write a word of the page, I write the architecture.

George Miller published "The Magical Number Seven, Plus or Minus Two" in The Psychological Review in 1956. The paper demonstrated that human working memory can hold approximately seven items simultaneously. Subsequent research by Nelson Cowan in 2001 revised the estimate downward to four, plus or minus one. A skilled copywriter can hold three or four cognitive mechanisms in mind while writing. The Truth Font: keep it simple. Social Proof: add a testimonial. Urgency: create a deadline. That is the ceiling. Not a skill ceiling. A hardware ceiling. Human working memory has walls.

The architecture puts the mechanisms on the other side of those walls, in a document the AI reads before it generates a single word.

THE AI DEPLOYMENT ARCHITECTURE

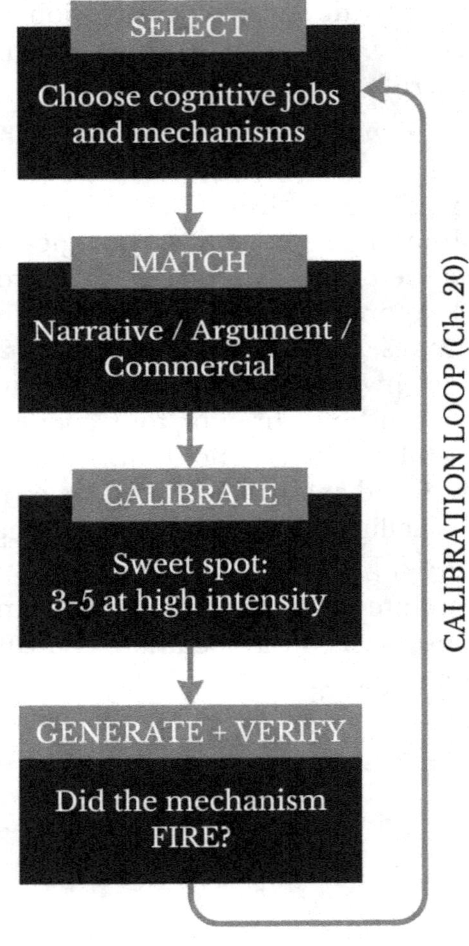

The machine deploys. The loop calibrates.

Step One: Select the Cognitive Jobs and Mechanisms

This page must do all six jobs. Here is how I select mechanisms for each one.

For CAPTURE, I select The Truth Font and The Open Loop. The headline must be short (fluency) and must create a question (gap). I instruct the AI: "Write a headline of 8 words or fewer that poses a question the reader needs answered about their email marketing. Do not describe the course. Create a gap."

The AI generates: "Why do your best emails get ignored?"

Seven words. Fluent. The reader who sends emails needs to know the answer. The gap is open.

For ENGAGE, I select The Push-Pull and the Completion Impulse. The first section must create tension between wanting better results and fearing the effort required. I instruct: "Write two paragraphs. The first describes the frustration of low open rates in specific, recognizable terms. The second hints that the fix is simpler than the reader expects. Create simultaneous desire and skepticism."

For TRUST, I select Pratfall and Specificity. I instruct: "Include one sentence where the course creator admits a specific email marketing mistake they made, with the exact date and consequence. Follow with three specific, named data points about email marketing effectiveness."

For WANT, I select Reactance and Status Quo Bias Exploit. I instruct: "Frame the course as available only until Friday. Then quantify the cost of the reader's current approach: how many hours per month they spend writing emails that underperform, and what that time is worth at their billing rate."

For ACT, I select The Truth Font. I instruct: "The CTA button is four words or fewer. The sentence immediately before the button validates the reader's frustration and offers the resolution in one clause."

For BOND, I select Vocabulary Gift. I instruct: "The final paragraph introduces one framework name the reader can use in their own email marketing tomorrow, even if they do not buy the course."

Six jobs. Twelve mechanisms selected. The instruction document is 200 words. The AI has not written anything yet.

Step Two: Match the Mode

Each mechanism deploys differently depending on whether the content is narrative (fiction), argument (nonfiction), or commercial (marketing). This page is commercial. That changes the deployment.

The Truth Font in fiction means the lies are written simply and the truth is written with friction. The Truth Font in nonfiction means core claims are the simplest sentences in the chapter. The Truth Font in commercial means the CTA is the shortest line on the page. Same mechanism. Different expression.

For this page, mode matching produces specific instructions. The Open Loop in commercial mode is not an intellectual puzzle (that is argument mode). It is a felt question: why are my emails failing? The Push-Pull is not a character dilemma (that is narrative mode). It is the reader's own tension between wanting better results and fearing the effort of learning something new. The Pratfall is not the author's intellectual error (that is argument mode). It is a business mistake with a dollar figure attached.

I add mode-specific notes to each mechanism instruction. The document is now 350 words.

Step Three: Calibrate Density

This is where most people get the deployment wrong. More mechanisms is not always better.

The lesson from Chapter 9 applies here: a sales page that deploys all forty-six mechanisms simultaneously does not feel persuasive. It feels like a carnival barker. The reader's authenticity detector fires. The content trips the Behavioral Uncanny Valley.

The density calibration follows a principle I learned by running hundreds of variations through the system: three to five mechanisms at high intensity per piece of content, with the remaining mechanisms either at low intensity or absent. A landing page that deploys The Truth Font, The Open Loop, Identifiable Victim, Anchoring, and Commitment Escalation at full intensity will outperform a page that tries to layer in all forty-six. Density without hierarchy produces noise.

For this page, I set high intensity on three mechanisms: The Truth Font (at the CTA), The Open Loop (at the headline), and Reactance (at the pricing section). Medium intensity on Pratfall, The Push-Pull, and Vocabulary Gift. The remaining six are at low intensity or absent.

I add density levels to the instruction document. It is now 450 words. The AI still has not written the page.

Step Four: Generate and Verify

Now the AI writes. It receives the architecture document and generates the page. I read the output. Not for grammar. Not for tone. For mechanism execution.

Did The Open Loop make me curious? The headline reads: "Why do your best emails get ignored?" Yes. I want the answer.

Did the Pratfall feel genuine? The AI wrote: "In March 2023, I sent a campaign to 4,200 subscribers that I thought was my best work. Open rate: 11%. I had written the subject line at midnight after three revisions. Every revision made it worse." It reads like a real admission. Not calculated. Specific enough to be credible. The date, the number, the detail about midnight revisions. Pass.

Is the CTA the simplest sentence on the page? "Start the course." Three words. Surrounded by longer sentences in the pricing section. The fluency contrast is visible. Pass.

Did the Vocabulary Gift land as useful? The closing paragraph introduces a term: "The Subject Line Audit." It is a three-question test the reader can apply to their next email without buying the course. The term is specific, actionable, and usable in conversation. "I ran a Subject Line Audit on my last campaign." Pass.

But The Push-Pull section reads flat. The AI described the frustration of low open rates in generic terms. "Many business owners struggle with email engagement." That is not The Push-Pull. That is a category description. I rewrite the instruction for that section: "Describe the specific moment when a business owner checks their email analytics the morning after a campaign and sees the open rate. The wanting: the hope that this time it worked. The fearing: the knowledge that it probably did not. Use second person. Put the reader in the moment."

The AI regenerates that section. The new version: "You know the feeling. You sent the campaign last night. You open the dashboard at 7 AM with your coffee still too hot to drink, and the number is right there. Fourteen percent. You did not expect fifty. But you expected more than fourteen."

The Push-Pull is now operating. The reader wants better results and fears confirming that their current approach is not working. The oscillation is present.

I do not rewrite the entire page. I identify which mechanism failed and rewrite the instruction for that section only. The architecture tells me exactly where the failure is and what to fix. I am not guessing. I am diagnosing.

The Same Architecture, Different Surfaces

The sales page walkthrough above is one content type. The architecture works the same way across any surface. Two brief examples.

A B2B consulting pitch deck. The client is a management consulting firm. The deck has 12 slides. Before the architecture: the deck opened with "About Us" (no CAPTURE), moved through capabilities (no ENGAGE), listed case studies (weak TRUST, no identifiable victim), and ended with pricing (no WANT, no ACT bridge). After the architecture: Slide 1 deploys The Open Loop ("Your competitors reduced client churn by 34%. You can see their strategy. You cannot see why it worked."). Slide 4 deploys a single Identifiable Victim case study instead of four generic ones. Slide 11 deploys the Implementation Bridge ("The audit takes one week. We start Monday."). The content changed by maybe 15 percent. The structure changed entirely.

A YouTube video hook. The creator makes videos about productivity. The first three seconds must deploy CAPTURE before the viewer scrolls. Before the architecture: "In this video I'm going to show you five productivity tips." After the architecture: "I tracked every minute of my day for 30 days. On day 17, I found the hour that was killing my productivity." The revised hook deploys The Open Loop (what happened on day 17?), Specificity (30 days, day 17), and The Mirror Moment (the viewer has also wondered where their time goes). Three mechanisms in three seconds. The AI instruction for this hook was 40 words.

The architecture does not care about the medium. It cares about the cognitive jobs. A pitch deck, a YouTube hook, and a sales page all need CAPTURE. The mechanisms that serve CAPTURE operate the same way in all three. The deployment differs. The architecture is constant.

Mechanism Stacking: What Happens When They Interact

When multiple mechanisms operate in a single piece of content, they interact. Some combinations amplify each other. Others cancel.

I call the deliberate layering of multiple mechanisms in a single content unit Mechanism Stacking, and it is the practice that separates content built on the architecture from content built on instinct.

An email subject line: "What your competitors learned about pricing last Tuesday (and why they are not sharing it)." Count the mechanisms. The Truth Font: the sentence is short and readable. The Open Loop: the reader does not know what competitors learned. Reactance: the implication of withheld information triggers the autonomy drive. Temporal Landmark: "last Tuesday" is specific and concrete. Specificity: "pricing," not "business strategy." Five mechanisms in a single sentence. Each one amplifies the others. The fluency makes the gap feel real. The gap makes the reactance feel urgent. The reactance makes the temporal landmark feel timely.

MECHANISM STACKING

One email subject line, five mechanisms

What your competitors learned about pricing last Tuesday (and why they aren't sharing it)

1. **The Truth Font** → *"What"*
   Short, readable opening
2. **The Open Loop** → *"learned"*
   Reader doesn't know what was learned
3. **The Velvet Rope** → *"aren't sharing it"*
   Withheld information triggers resistance to being excluded
4. **The Timestamp** → *"last Tuesday"*
   Specific and concrete, not vague
5. **Specificity** → *"pricing"*
   Not "business strategy" -- one precise topic

Compare: "5 Pricing Tips for Your Business" -- one mechanism at best.

Each mechanism amplifies the others. The Truth Font makes the gap feel real. The gap makes The Velvet Rope urgent.

Compare: "5 Pricing Tips for Your Business." One mechanism at best (weak fluency). No gap. No reactance. No specificity. No temporal anchor. The subject line is not bad. It is architecture-free. It relies on the reader's pre-existing interest in pricing tips, which is a bet that loses more often than it wins.

The Visual Layer

The architecture operates on language first, on the sentences the AI generates. But there is a second channel the brain encodes through, and leaving it out is the most common mistake I see in architecture-informed content.

Allan Paivio published Dual Coding Theory in 1971 and expanded it through 1991. The claim: the brain encodes information through two independent but interconnected channels, verbal and visual, and information represented in both is remembered far better than information represented in either alone. In 1973, Lionel Standing tested the ceiling. Subjects were shown ten thousand images over five days. On a recognition test afterward, they identified the images they had seen with 83 percent accuracy. Ten thousand. Not a list of words. Images. Richard Mayer's three decades of multimedia learning research have confirmed the effect across educational and commercial contexts. The Picture Print is one of the most replicated mechanisms in cognitive psychology.

This book has been deploying it on you since Chapter 1.

The Master Map diagram in Chapter 1 is not decoration. Forty-six mechanisms organized across six cognitive jobs is a large amount of information to hold in working memory. Miller's seven, Cowan's four, either way the verbal description of the architecture will not survive the chapter boundary without help. The diagram provides the visual imprint. The verbal explanation is the textual channel. Both channels encode the same architecture, which is why a reader can recall the six cognitive jobs a week after closing the book even when they cannot reproduce the exact definitions of individual mechanisms. Verbal alone decays. Paired with visual, it persists.

AI-era deployment extends the mechanism. Modern AI systems generate images alongside text. A prompt for a sales page should produce not just the copy but the hero image, the infographic, the icon set, each one engineered to the same cognitive job the text is serving. The Mechanism Stacking example from the prior section lands harder when paired with a visual that dramatizes the five stacked mechanisms. The Vocabulary Gift closing section becomes stickier when the named framework is also a diagram the reader can screenshot and save.

The instruction that changes in architecture-informed AI deployment: do not generate the image after the text is written. Generate it from the same cognitive-job specification. If the text is carrying CAPTURE through The Open Loop, the image should also carry CAPTURE, through composition that leaves a question unresolved. If the text is carrying BOND through the Vocabulary Gift, the image should be the visual form of the named framework, repeatable and screenshot-friendly.

The architecture is not a text layer. It is a content layer. Text and image are two channels. Deploy the mechanism on both.

External Validation

I have been describing my own system. The reasonable question is whether anyone else has demonstrated the same principle at scale.

Persado, an AI content optimization platform based in New York, published their 2023 annual impact report documenting performance across more than 150,000 AI-generated marketing messages for clients including JPMorgan Chase, Vodafone, and Air Canada. Their finding: messages that were structured around what they call "motivation-based language models," which map emotional and cognitive triggers to specific message elements, outperformed unstructured AI-generated messages by 41 percent in conversion rate. Persado's system classifies language into categories that map recognizably to the cognitive jobs: urgency (ACT), exclusivity (WANT/Reactance), achievement (identity signaling), and gratitude (BOND). Their framework uses different terminology than the Influence Architecture. The principle is identical: AI content that is architecturally informed by cognitive science outperforms AI content generated through pattern completion alone.

JPMorgan Chase signed a five-year deal with Persado in 2019 after a pilot in which Persado's cognitively structured ad copy outperformed JPMorgan's human-written copy in 99 percent of A/B tests. Not by marginal amounts. By double-digit percentage improvements in click-through rates across digital marketing campaigns reaching millions of customers. The bank's CMO at the time, Kristin Lemkau, told The Financial Brand that the results were "not even close."

The Human's Irreducible Role

I need to be direct about what the machine cannot do, because overpromising on AI is the fastest way to undermine the credibility this book has spent nineteen chapters building.

As of early 2026, AI systems can deploy cognitive mechanisms with remarkable consistency when given clear architectural instructions. They can maintain The Truth Font across a 60,000-word manuscript. They can track Commitment Escalation across twenty chapters. They can deploy Mirror Moments that make readers recognize their own behavior.

What they cannot do is evaluate whether those deployments worked.

A deployed mechanism that is technically present but emotionally inert is worse than no deployment at all. A pratfall that reads as calculated is not a pratfall. It is a manipulation that the reader detects and punishes. A self-reference moment that describes generic behavior instead of the specific, slightly embarrassing, universally true behavior that triggers recognition is not a Mirror Moment. It is a sentence that takes up space.

The human's irreplaceable role is judgment. Not creation. Not execution. Judgment. Did the narrative transportation put you in the room? Did the schema violation genuinely surprise you? Did the identifiable victim make you feel something? These questions cannot be answered by the system that produced the content. They require a reader. A human reader, with a human brain, running on the same forty-six mechanisms the architecture is designed to deploy.

The architecture does not replace the human. It gives the human the right question to ask: not "is this well written?" but "which cognitive jobs does this accomplish, and did the mechanisms fire?"

The machine can deploy all forty-six. The reader now has the architecture. But there is one thing left. One question the book has been setting up since page one. What happens when you look back at this book not as a source of information, but as a deployment? What if the proof of concept was not described in these pages, but demonstrated in them?

Deploy It Now (3 minutes)

Open the last piece you published, sent, or delivered. Write six labels down the left margin of a page: CAPTURE, ENGAGE, TRUST, WANT, ACT, BOND. For each label, write a score from 0 to 3. Zero means the job is absent. One means it is present but weak. Two means it is working. Three means it would survive an audit.

Now circle the lowest score. That is not your weakest content. That is your missing cognitive job. Write one sentence describing what mechanism you would add to raise that score by one point. You do not need all forty-six mechanisms. You need the one that is at zero.

Chapter 20: The Calibration Loop

In January 2022, a team of researchers at OpenAI ran an experiment that should have been impossible.

They took a language model with 1.3 billion parameters, a system small enough that most AI labs would not bother publishing its results, and trained it using a three-step loop. First, the model generated outputs. Second, human evaluators ranked those outputs. Third, the model recalibrated its internal weights based on the rankings and generated again. Loop. Loop. Loop. The process consumed less than 2 percent of the computation that had been required to train the original model.

Then they tested it against GPT-3. The same GPT-3 that had stunned the AI world with its 175 billion parameters, its ability to generate coherent essays and working code, its sheer brute-force scale. GPT-3 had 134 times the raw computational power of this small, calibrated model.

Human evaluators preferred the small model 85 percent of the time.

Long Ouyang and his colleagues published the results at NeurIPS in 2022. The paper described InstructGPT, and the three-step training process was Reinforcement Learning from Human Feedback. The finding rewrote the rules of AI development: the calibration loop was worth more than a hundredfold increase in raw power. Not slightly better. Not marginally better. Preferred five out of six times against a model that dwarfed it.

The hallucination rate dropped from 41 percent to 21 percent. Toxic outputs fell by 25 percent. And the entire recalibration process used less than 2 percent of the resources that had built the larger model.

That ratio is the thesis of this chapter.

Why Static Frameworks Lose

Calibration beats scale. A system that deploys, measures, and adjusts will outperform a system with more knowledge, more resources, and more sophistication that cannot learn from its own output. This is not a motivational claim. It is an engineering fact with a specific evidence base.

And it is the single most important difference between the Influence Architecture and every persuasion framework that came before it.

Robert Cialdini published *Influence: The Psychology of Persuasion* in 1984. Six principles. They were correct, well-evidenced, and immediately useful. In 2016, thirty-two years later, he published *Pre-Suasion* and added a seventh: Unity. Two updates in thirty-two years.

Cialdini's framework is a photograph. Clear, sharp, captured at the moment of its creation. It cannot observe its own effects. It cannot measure which principle worked in a given campaign. It cannot adjust the weight of Reciprocity relative to Scarcity for a specific audience. It sits on a shelf and waits for the practitioner to pick it up, deploy it by instinct, and never report back.

The Influence Architecture does not sit on a shelf. It generates feedback after every deployment cycle, adjusts the weights of all forty-six mechanisms, and starts the next iteration from a better baseline. That is not a feature of the system. It is the system.

A photograph does not compete with a feedback loop.

The Four-Stage Cycle

The Calibration Loop has four stages. Each one feeds the next, and the cycle repeats.

Stage 1: Deploy. Produce content with weighted mechanisms. Not binary, deploy-or-not. Weighted. Each of the forty-six mechanisms has an intensity setting from 1 to 10, like channels on a mixing board. A thriller manuscript weights Narrative Transportation at 9 and Vocabulary Gift at 2. A business book weights The Truth Font at 8 and The Reminiscence Bump at 2. A fundraising email weights the Identifiable Victim Effect at 10 and Reactance at 1. The weights are the architecture. Two practitioners using the same forty-six mechanisms with different weights will produce entirely different content.

I call this the Mixing Board. Forty-six channels. Each with a slider. The output is not determined by which mechanisms you know. It is determined by where the sliders are set.

THE MIXING BOARD

Same 46 Mechanisms, Different Weights

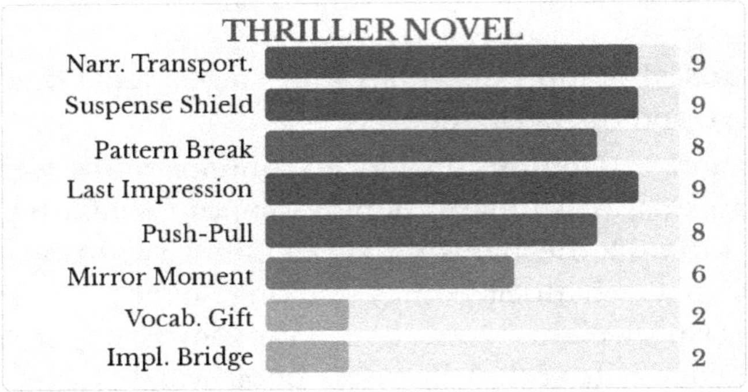

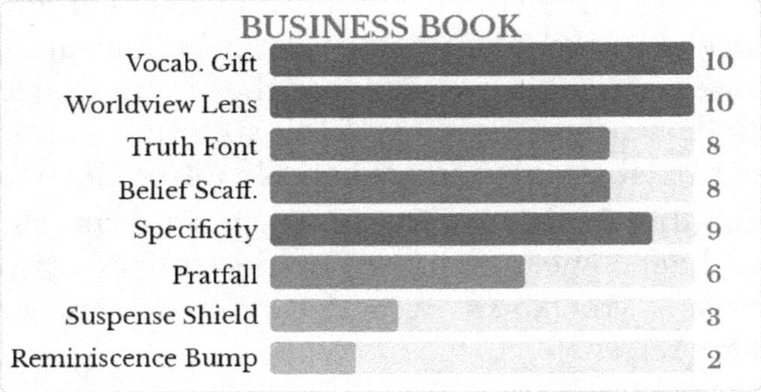

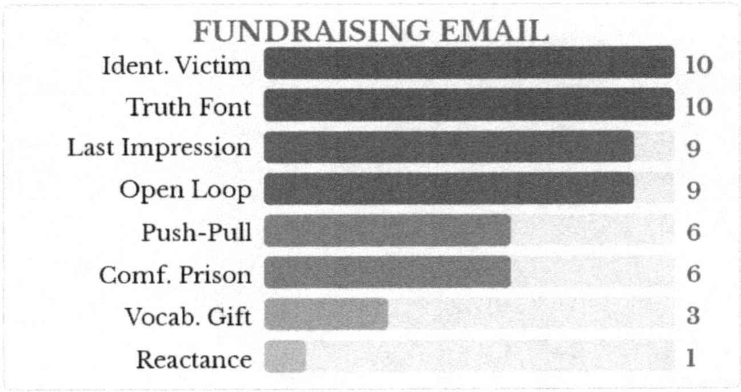

The output is not determined by which mechanisms you know. It is determined by where the sliders are set.

Stage 2: Measure. Collect feedback. This comes from two sources, and the distinction between them matters. Simulated feedback arrives before publication: AI reader personas score the manuscript against the six cognitive jobs. "CAPTURE scored 8.2 but ACT scored 5.4. The implementation bridge is weak." This is the dress rehearsal. Real feedback arrives after publication: Amazon reviews mined for mechanism signals. Email open rates mapped to subject-line mechanism stacking. YouTube retention graphs showing second-by-second where attention dropped. Instagram saves revealing which mechanisms drove sharing. The algorithm is already measuring which mechanisms worked. The data is sitting in your analytics dashboard. You just did not know what to look for.

Stage 3: Diagnose. Which mechanisms landed? Which were technically present but emotionally inert? Which backfired? A Pratfall Effect that reads as calculated instead of genuine is not a pratfall. It is a manipulation the reader detected. An Open Loop that the reader did not notice is not a gap. It is a sentence that occupies space. The diagnostic stage separates mechanisms that fired from mechanisms that were merely present.

Stage 4: Calibrate. Adjust the weights for the next iteration. Not by gut feeling. By signal. If the TRUST job scored high but the ACT job scored low, increase the weight on Implementation Bridge and Commitment Escalation for the next deployment. If read-through rate dropped in Chapter 12, examine which mechanisms were underweighted in that chapter relative to the chapters where retention held. The calibration is specific, measurable, and tied to data. Then deploy again. Not from zero. Not from the same weights as last time. From a baseline that incorporates everything the previous cycle learned. The arrow from Calibrate points back to Deploy.

The loop closes. The gap between the first iteration and the tenth is the gap between competent content and content that changes behavior.

THE CALIBRATION LOOP

Static frameworks are published and frozen.
The Influence Architecture learns.

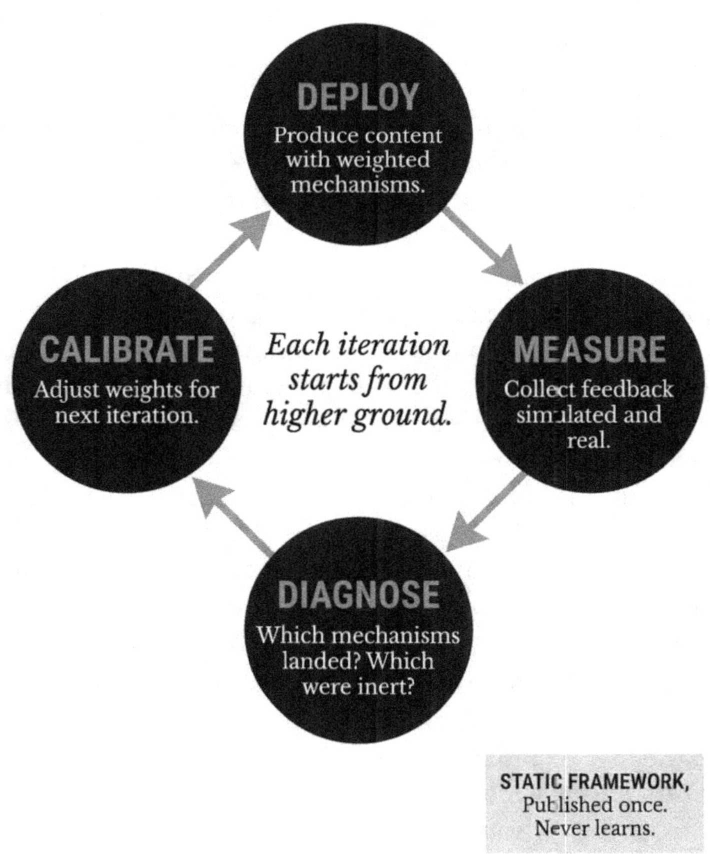

Deploy. Measure. Diagnose. Calibrate. Repeat.

Forty-Four Million Games

The purest proof of the calibration loop did not come from marketing. It came from chess.

In 2017, a team at DeepMind led by David Silver built a system called AlphaZero. They gave it the rules of chess. Nothing else. No opening theory. No endgame tables. No database of grandmaster games. No human knowledge of any kind. They pointed it at a chessboard and told it to play against itself.

AlphaZero played 44 million games in nine hours.

Each game generated a tiny feedback signal: win, lose, or draw. The system adjusted its internal weights after each batch of games. It played millions more. Adjusted again. Played again.

After four hours, AlphaZero surpassed Stockfish, the strongest conventional chess engine in the world. Stockfish had been built by teams of programmers encoding decades of grandmaster knowledge into handcrafted evaluation functions, a static framework refined by human experts over years. AlphaZero knew nothing about chess except the rules and the feedback. Silver and his colleagues published the results in *Science* in December 2018. In a 1,000-game match under tournament conditions, AlphaZero won 155 games, lost 6, and drew 839.

Here is the detail that stops me every time I read it. Stockfish evaluates 70 million chess positions per second. AlphaZero evaluates 80,000. A thousand-to-one difference in raw computational power. But the calibrated system, using a thousandth of the brute force, made better decisions. The loop substituted for scale.

The community-built open-source engine Leela Chess Zero replicated AlphaZero's methodology using volunteer hardware, confirming the result. And in 2022, a team of researchers published a study in the *Proceedings of the National Academy of Sciences* that analyzed what AlphaZero had learned and when. Using linear probes to examine the system's internal representations at each stage of training, they found that AlphaZero first learned material values (which pieces are worth more), then king safety, then positional concepts like space and mobility, then endgame theory. This is the same progression that human chess education follows. A system with no human input independently discovered the same learning sequence that centuries of chess pedagogy had converged on.

The calibration loop does not just optimize. It discovers the same knowledge structures that experts find valuable.

The Gap That Matters Is Not Knowledge

If the AlphaZero result were unique to chess, it would be a remarkable curiosity and nothing more. Chess is a perfect-information game with a binary outcome. Persuasion operates in noise, partial information, and ambiguous results. The question is whether calibration produces the same advantage in the messier domain of human influence.

In 2025, a meta-analysis published in *Scientific Reports* answered the question. The researchers aggregated seven studies involving 17,422 participants and twelve effect sizes, examining whether large language models were more or less persuasive than humans.

The overall effect: $g = 0.02$, not statistically significant. LLMs and humans are equally persuasive on average.

That finding sounds like a draw. It is the opposite.

The contextual factors in the analysis, the specific model used, the conversation design, the domain, and the calibration of deployment, explained 81.93 percent of the between-study variance. Not the raw persuasive power. Not the number of mechanisms available. The context. The calibration. The settings on the mixing board.

Raw mechanism knowledge is a wash. Every LLM has access to the same persuasion research. Every human marketer can read Cialdini. The difference between a persuasion deployment that works and one that does not is the same difference that separated InstructGPT from GPT-3: not what you know, but how you calibrate what you deploy.

Commercial Proof

Persado, the platform I described in Chapter 19, does not just deploy cognitively structured content. It runs the Calibration Loop. The results go beyond the 41 percent conversion improvement I cited there. Across their platform, Persado reported that calibrated content outperformed human-written and generic LLM content 96 percent of the time. JPMorgan Chase saw up to 450 percent lift in click-through rates during their pilot, which led to a five-year enterprise deal in July 2019. A top U.S. bank drove more than $1 billion in incremental revenue over four years using the system.

These numbers come from Persado's own published data, not from independent peer review. I note this because the evidence standard in this book requires it. But Chase does not sign five-year enterprise deals on the basis of inflated vendor statistics. The signal is strong.

The mechanism at work is the same one that separated AlphaZero from Stockfish and InstructGPT from GPT-3. Not more knowledge. Not more power. A loop.

Your Brain Already Runs This Algorithm

In 1997, Wolfram Schultz, Peter Dayan, and P. Read Montague published a paper in *Science* that identified the brain's native calibration loop. They recorded from dopamine neurons in primates and found that these neurons do not simply fire when a reward arrives. They fire based on the gap between the predicted reward and the actual reward. A reward that is better than expected produces a burst. A reward that matches the prediction produces nothing. A reward that is worse than expected produces a depression in firing.

If you read Chapter 3 of this book, you have encountered Schultz's prediction error before. In that chapter, it appeared as the mechanism behind Pattern-Break Dopamine: the surprise response that makes the brain flag unexpected information as important. Here it reappears in a different frame. The same neural signal that captures attention through surprise is, at a deeper level, the brain's own calibration system.

The prediction error signal is mathematically equivalent to the temporal difference algorithm used in reinforcement learning, the same family of algorithms that trained AlphaZero and InstructGPT. The brain does not passively store experience. It generates predictions, compares them against outcomes, computes the error, and updates its internal model. Every time. Automatically. From birth until death.

When a mechanism in the Influence Architecture lands stronger than expected (an Open Loop that the reader tracks for three pages), the system increases the weight of that mechanism for the next deployment. When a mechanism underperforms (a Pratfall that reads as calculated), the system decreases the weight. This is not a metaphor for how the brain works. It is the same algorithm running on different substrates. Silicon in one case. Dopamine neurons in the other.

The Frequency Paradox

Here is where I need to be honest about what the calibration loop cannot do.

In 1984, Alan Salmoni, Richard Schmidt, and Charles Walter published a review in *Psychological Bulletin* that upended the intuitive assumption about feedback in motor learning. The assumption was straightforward: more feedback produces faster learning. Feedback after every trial should outperform feedback after every other trial, which should outperform feedback after every fifth trial. More information, better calibration, faster improvement.

The data showed the opposite.

Reduced feedback frequency, specifically feedback on 50 percent of trials rather than 100 percent, produced greater long-term skill retention. Learners who received constant feedback performed better during the practice sessions but worse on retention tests. Learners who received intermittent feedback performed worse during practice but better when tested later.

The explanation cuts against every instinct about optimization. Constant feedback creates dependency. The learner stops developing internal error-detection capability because external feedback handles the error signal. Remove the feedback and the performance collapses. Intermittent feedback forces the learner to generate their own error signal, to develop what Salmoni's team called intrinsic error detection. The struggle IS the learning.

This finding has been replicated across dozens of motor learning studies. And it sets a critical boundary on the Calibration Loop.

The practitioner who recalibrates after every email, every social post, every individual piece of content, is not calibrating. They are creating dependency on external signal and preventing the development of their own judgment.

What does campaign-level calibration look like in practice? A content marketer runs a quarterly email campaign. After the sequence completes, they review the aggregate data: which emails had the highest open rates, which had the highest click-through, where did unsubscribes cluster. They map those signals back to the mechanism weights. The emails that opened well probably had strong CAPTURE (The Truth Font in the subject line, The Open Loop in the preview text). The emails that converted probably had strong ACT (Implementation Bridge, clean CTA). The emails that drove unsubscribes probably over-deployed Reactance or Urgency without earning TRUST first. The practitioner adjusts the weights for the next quarterly cycle. Not the next email. The next cycle.

A book author completes a manuscript. After publication, they review Amazon reviews, read-through rates, and reader feedback. They map the signals to chapters and mechanism deployments. The chapters where readers highlighted passages probably had strong Vocabulary Gift or Mirror Moments. The chapters where Kindle data shows readers slowing down or abandoning probably had a weak Open Loop or excessive density. The author adjusts weights for the next book. Not the next chapter revision. The next book.

The cadence matters. Calibrate after a product launch, a quarterly content cycle, a completed manuscript. At that scale, the signal is strong enough to be meaningful and infrequent enough to allow intrinsic judgment to develop alongside it. The practitioner who calibrates at campaign level develops both data literacy and taste. The practitioner who calibrates at the individual-content level develops neither.

Too much calibration is worse than not enough. The counterintuitive finding gives the system its boundary.

The Ten-Minute Version

Not every reader has an AI deployment system. Not every reader needs one.

The full Calibration Loop, with all forty-six mechanism weights measured and adjusted through simulated reader feedback and post-publish analytics, requires the architecture described in the previous chapter. But a simplified version requires nothing except the framework you already have.

The six-job audit from Chapter 16: pull up the last piece of content you published and evaluate it against CAPTURE, ENGAGE, TRUST, WANT, ACT, and BOND. Which jobs are present? Which are missing? Write your answers in the margins. That document, with your annotations, is the input for your next iteration. You have just run the Calibration Loop. No AI required. Ten minutes.

The loop does not require forty-six channels and a mixing board. It requires the willingness to measure your own output against a standard and adjust. The mixing board is the professional version. The six-job audit is where everyone starts.

What the Architecture Becomes

The Influence Architecture, as presented in the first nineteen chapters, is a catalog. Forty-six mechanisms organized by six cognitive jobs, with evidence, deployment patterns, and an AI execution layer. That is what the book has described.

But a catalog does not improve. The Calibration Loop transforms the catalog into a living system. Each deployment generates data. Each data point informs the next deployment. Each iteration starts from a baseline that the previous iteration could not have achieved. The gap between a static framework and a calibrated architecture is not a gap in knowledge. It is a gap in kind.

The architecture deploys. The loop calibrates. Each iteration starts from higher ground. But there is one question this book has been building toward since page one. A question about the book you are holding right now. What if the proof of concept was not described in these pages, but demonstrated in them?

Deploy It Now (3 minutes)

Pull up your last completed sequence. Not a single piece. A sequence: an email series, a lecture arc, a launch cycle, a month of content, a fundraising campaign Identify the entry that performed best and the one that performed worst by whatever metric matters to you.

For the winner, name the one mechanism you believe drove the result. For the loser, name the one mechanism that was missing or misfired. Write both down. That pair of observations is your first calibration signal. Adjust one weight for the next cycle: increase the mechanism that won, decrease or replace the one that lost. One adjustment per cycle. Not twelve. One.

Chapter 21: The Chapter That Used Every Technique on You

Karen Blackwell had done everything right.

You read that sentence twenty chapters ago. You remember it. Not because it was particularly clever. Because it was the first sentence of a case study about a marketing director whose campaign was respectable, professional, and forgettable, and you recognized something in her story before you could name what you were recognizing.

In Chapter 1, you watched Karen Blackwell deploy three mechanisms against Daniel Schreiber's twelve. You watched the architecture gap produce a 4x conversion difference. You nodded. You thought: I know the feeling. I have been Blackwell. I have read the books. I have known the principles. And I have watched better-architected campaigns outperform mine without understanding why.

That recognition was not an accident.

It was IA-02: The Mirror Moment. The mechanism that causes the brain to encode self-relevant information two to three times more deeply than information about other people. Karen Blackwell was designed to be you. Her credentials were your credentials. Her shelf of persuasion books was your shelf. Her confidence was your confidence. And her failure was the failure you have felt but never had a framework to explain.

You have been inside the proof of concept since page one.

What the Architecture Looked Like from the Builder's Side

I need to show you something. Not a new mechanism. Not a new case study. Something about this book. About what it was doing while you were reading it.

This book was not a description of the Influence Architecture. It was a deployment of it. Every chapter was designed not just to teach a mechanism but to demonstrate it on you, the reader, in real time. The teaching was real. The science was real. The case studies were real. And underneath all of it, the architecture was operating.

Not all forty-six mechanisms in every chapter. That would be the carnival barker from Chapter 9. The deployment was curated. Selective. Each chapter had a primary mechanism assignment, a density calibration, and a specific cognitive job it served in the book's overall sequence. The book followed its own architecture: CAPTURE in the first four chapters, ENGAGE in the next four, TRUST in the next three, WANT in the next three, ACT in two, and BOND in two. The sequence you read was not a table of contents. It was the architecture in action.

Here is what it looked like from inside the control room.

The Fluency Proof

Chapter 2 taught you that simple prose feels true. The brain uses processing ease as a truth heuristic, and information presented in clean, short sentences is rated as more likely to be correct than identical information in complex sentences. Reber and Schwarz. The University of Michigan. 1999.

While you were learning this, the chapter was doing it.

Chapter 2 was written in the simplest, most fluent prose in the manuscript. Shorter average sentences than any other chapter. Simpler syntax. Fewer subordinate clauses. The core claim of the chapter landed in a sentence structure that your fluency heuristic rated as true before your analytical mind had time to evaluate the evidence.

You did not notice the prose style was different from the chapters around it. Your brain noticed. The Truth Font was not described in that chapter. It was the chapter.

And then I told you I had gotten it wrong. The pratfall. Six months of producing "the most fluent nonsense you have ever read" before understanding that fluency without substance is decoration, not architecture. That admission was IA-12, the Pratfall Effect, deployed in the Look Inside window where Amazon shows potential buyers the first three chapters. A competent author who admits a failure in the first fifty pages earns more trust than an author who projects expertise without seams.

The pratfall was real. The placement was architectural. The trust you felt after reading it was the mechanism at work.

The Pattern That Broke

Chapter 3 opened differently. You noticed.

Chapters 1 and 2 both opened with named people in specific moments: Karen Blackwell in her Hartford conference room, Reber and Schwarz in their Michigan lab. You had absorbed a pattern. Named person, specific place, unfolding narrative. Your brain built a prediction model: this is how chapters in this book start.

Chapter 3 violated the prediction. It opened with a cold data point. No person. No narrative setup. A number, isolated on the page.

The absence of the expected structure was the lesson. Your prediction model expected a story. It got a number. The mismatch triggered the same prediction-error dopamine that Wolfram Schultz documented in his 1997 primate research. The structural outlier was remembered. The mechanism you were learning about, Pattern-Break Dopamine, was the mechanism being deployed on you.

You may have thought: that chapter felt different. It did. On purpose. The feeling was the proof.

The Moment You Saw Yourself

Chapter 7 was the deployment I am most uncertain about and most proud of.

"You have rehearsed a conversation in the shower that you will never have. You have checked your phone for a notification you know has not arrived. You have opened the refrigerator and stared into it as though the contents might change."

Those sentences were not observations about human behavior in general. They were about you. Specifically.

Rogers, Kuiper, and Kirker demonstrated in 1977 that self-relevant information encodes at two to three times the depth of non-self-relevant information. Symons and Johnson confirmed it across 129 studies in 1997. The science is solid.

But the science is not what made that moment work. What made it work was the specificity. Not "people sometimes engage in absent-minded behavior." That is a textbook sentence. Nobody recognizes themselves in a textbook sentence. "You have opened the refrigerator and stared into it as though the contents might change." That is a private behavior. Universally true and rarely written. The specificity of the description is what triggers the medial prefrontal cortex to tag the information as self-relevant. The brain does not activate self-reference circuits for generic claims about human nature. It activates them for descriptions of things you have actually done, described with enough precision that you cannot pretend the passage is about someone else.

The most powerful sentence you will ever write is the one that makes a stranger think: that's me.

If you are reading this and thinking "I did recognize myself in that passage," you have just confirmed the mechanism a second time. This paragraph is also deploying The Mirror Moment. The layer goes as deep as you are willing to look.

The Admission That Built Trust

In Chapter 9, I told you about the worst marketing I have ever produced. The AI-generated sales pages that read like a carnival barker at a county fair. Every sentence selling. Every paragraph escalating. The content tripped the Behavioral Uncanny Valley because it deployed too many mechanisms at too high an intensity without the imperfection that signals authenticity.

That story was true. It was also strategically placed.

The Pratfall Effect, documented by Elliot Aronson in 1966, shows that a competent person who reveals a genuine flaw is rated as more likeable and more credible than a competent person who presents without flaws. The effect is specific: the person must be demonstrably competent before the pratfall. Incompetent people who make mistakes are just incompetent. Competent people who make mistakes are human.

By Chapter 9, you had spent eight chapters watching me present research accurately, name studies with precision, and build a framework with coherence. The competence was established. The pratfall, arriving against that baseline, did not undermine credibility. It compounded it. You trusted me more after the admission than before. And you trusted the mechanisms the book was teaching because the author demonstrated the willingness to tell you when he had deployed them badly.

The progression was deliberate. Chapter 2 contained a smaller pratfall: six months of fluent nonsense. A minor failure, in the Look Inside window, that established the author as human. Chapter 9 escalated the vulnerability: the carnival barker confession, deeper, more embarrassing, more instructive. The trust you gave me in Chapter 2 made the deeper admission in Chapter 9 possible. The scaffolding of vulnerability mirrors the scaffolding of belief.

The Title That Made You Read

Chapter 12 was called "The Freedom You Can't Have." You read it. The title is the reason.

Jack Brehm's 1966 reactance research demonstrated that restricting access to an option increases desire for that option. The mechanism is pre-conscious. It does not require agreement. The mere framing of information as restricted, exclusive, or forbidden triggers the autonomy drive. You did not decide to read Chapter 12 because the title was informative. You read it because the title implied restriction, and the restriction made you want what was being withheld.

The chapter title was a one-sentence deployment of the mechanism the chapter taught. The Velvet Rope was the reading motivation and the lesson. You experienced the mechanism and then learned its name.

The Vocabulary You Carry

Here is a test. Without going back to look, list the six cognitive jobs.

You can do it. CAPTURE, ENGAGE, TRUST, WANT, ACT, BOND. They came to you without effort. You did not memorize them. You absorbed them through repeated use across twenty chapters, each one reinforcing the framework until the vocabulary became part of how you process information.

That absorption is IA-41, the Vocabulary Gift. Chapter 13 named it explicitly, but the mechanism had been operating since Chapter 1. Every time you encountered the six jobs, the vocabulary deepened. Every time you applied it to a case study before I applied it for you, the vocabulary became yours. You own CAPTURE, ENGAGE, TRUST, WANT, ACT, and BOND the way you own "sunk cost fallacy" or "confirmation bias." They are part of your analytical toolkit now.

And here is the commercial reality of that ownership. The next time you are in a meeting and someone presents a marketing campaign, you will evaluate it through the six jobs. You will say: "The CAPTURE is strong but the TRUST job is empty. There is no specificity in the first scroll." Your colleague will ask what you mean. You will explain. You will name the book. Every use of the vocabulary is an unpaid recommendation.

The vocabulary was a gift. It was also architecture.

What "the Architecture" Means Now

I used the word "architecture" in Chapter 1. It meant something abstract. A concept. A gap between what Blackwell had and what Schreiber had. Something that existed in someone else's campaign.

I used it in Chapter 10. It meant something different. An evidence question. Could you trust the foundations? Were the studies real? The replication crisis chapter examined whether the science underneath the architecture deserved your belief. The architecture had shifted from aspiration to credibility test.

I used it in Chapter 17. It meant something richer. The Bonding Loop, The Reset cycles, The Loaded Word layering across touchpoints. The architecture was no longer a concept or a question. It was becoming the structure of the reader's own understanding.

I used it in Chapter 19. It meant a deployable system. Specific, technical, instructable to machines. The architecture had dimensions and a user manual. The four-step deployment. The mechanism stacking. The quality verification loop.

I used it in Chapter 20. It meant a living system. The Calibration Loop. Forty-six channels on a mixing board, each slider adjustable based on feedback. The architecture was no longer static. It learned. It improved. Each iteration started from a baseline the previous iteration could not have reached. The gap between the architecture and Cialdini's seven principles was no longer a gap in knowledge. It was a gap in kind. A photograph versus a feedback loop.

I am using it now. And the word carries all six meanings at once. The abstraction. The evidence. The bonding pattern. The deployable system. The learning system. But it carries something else too. Something that was not in the word twenty chapters ago.

You were inside it.

The architecture was not something described in these pages. It was the pages. The chapter sequence was the cognitive job sequence. The fluency of Chapter 2 was The Truth Font. The structural break of Chapter 3 was The Pattern Break. The recognition of Chapter 7 was The Mirror Moment. The admission of Chapter 9 was the Pratfall Effect. The restricted title of Chapter 12 was The Velvet Rope. The vocabulary you absorbed was the Vocabulary Gift. The return to Blackwell in this paragraph is narrative closure, the same mechanism that makes the final scene of a film return to the opening image and transform its meaning.

You did not read about the architecture. You lived in it. For twenty chapters, the proof of concept was not described. It was demonstrated. And the demonstration was your experience.

THE SIX COGNITIVE JOBS AS A BOOK MAP

CAPTURE *(Ch 1-4)*

Get noticed. Fluency, pattern-break, anchoring, specificity.

ENGAGE *(Ch 5-8)*

Hold attention. Cognitive gaps, approach-avoidance, self-reference.

TRUST *(Ch 9-11)*

Earn credibility. Pratfall, replication honesty, identifiable victim.

WANT *(Ch 12-14)*

Create desire. The Velvet Rope, The Badge, The Dissonance Trap.

ACT *(Ch 15-16)*

Drive conversion. The gap only your product fills.

BOND *(Ch 17-18)*

Build retention. The Bonding Loop, The Attachment Map.

THE ARCHITECTURE *(Ch 19-21)*

The machine, the loop, the reveal.

The chapter sequence was not a table of contents. It was the architecture in action.

That is what the word means now. It means all of it. Every chapter. Every mechanism you felt before you could name it. Every moment where something in the prose made you lean forward or see yourself or trust the author a little more. The architecture.

The Scaffolding You Were Standing On

There is one more layer.

In Chapter 1, I asked you to agree that there was a gap between deploying three or four mechanisms and deploying all forty-six. You agreed. The gap was obvious once you saw the Lemonade numbers.

In Chapter 2, I asked you to agree that The Truth Font changes whether the brain evaluates a claim as true. You agreed. The Reber and Schwarz data was compelling.

In Chapter 5, I asked you to agree that The Open Loop holds attention. In Chapter 7, that The Mirror Moment encodes more deeply. In Chapter 10, that the replication crisis matters and honest engagement with it builds trust. In Chapter 12, that restriction creates desire. In Chapter 14, that knowing without doing creates dissonance.

Each agreement was small. Each was backed by evidence. Each felt independent.

They were not independent. They were a sequence. The Staircase — Commitment Escalation, documented by Festinger and his colleagues — operates through consistency pressure: each small agreement makes the next one easier because the brain prefers internal coherence over contradiction. By Chapter 14, you had made thirteen consecutive agreements with the book's argument. Disagreeing with the fourteenth required questioning all thirteen that preceded it.

You did not feel manipulated. You felt convinced. The distinction matters. Manipulation is engineering belief without evidence. Architecture is engineering the

SEQUENCE of evidence so each piece lands with maximum cognitive force. Every claim in this book was backed by named research. Every mechanism was supported by specific studies. The evidence was real. The sequence of the evidence was the architecture.

And the belief scaffolding reached further than individual chapters. In Part I, you agreed that automatic systems operate before conscious evaluation. In Part II, that tension can be engineered. In Part III, that vulnerability and specificity earn credibility. In Part IV, that desire is created by restriction and identity, not by listing benefits. In Parts V and VI, that conversion and retention are architectural problems. Each agreement built on the last. By this chapter, the scaffold is so tall that the starting position, "persuasion is talent plus a few principles," is visible far below you. You did not climb here in a single step. You were built here, agreement by agreement, across a structure you are only now seeing from above.

The Cost of Knowing

There is something this book has taken from you. I should be honest about it.

Before Chapter 1, you could produce content casually. You could write an email without evaluating which cognitive jobs it accomplished. You could look at a landing page without seeing the missing mechanisms. You could watch a commercial without tagging the architecture. You could operate on instinct and three or four principles and never feel what was missing.

That comfort is gone.

You will see the architecture now. In your own emails. In your competitors' campaigns. In the charity appeals that make you reach for your wallet. In the book descriptions that make you click "Buy Now." In the political speeches that make you nod before you have evaluated the evidence. The framework is installed. It operates whether you want it to or not.

That is the cost of knowing. The comfortable ignorance of deploying three mechanisms by instinct is no longer available to you. It left somewhere around Chapter 7, when you recognized yourself in the refrigerator passage and realized this book was not teaching you about other people. It was teaching you about yourself.

And every piece of content you produce from now on carries the knowledge of what it could have deployed. The email you send tomorrow will pass through a filter you did not have three hundred pages ago. The landing page you review next week will be evaluated against the six cognitive jobs. The campaign you approve next month will remind you of the gap between what it is and what the architecture could make it.

This is not a comfortable feeling. It is the feeling of competence. The surgeon who understands every step of a procedure carries every step. The pilot who understands every system in the cockpit feels the gravity of every decision. The practitioner who understands the architecture sees the gaps everywhere, in their own work first.

The gap between knowledge and action is the Knowing-Deploying Gap, and it is the final mechanism this book deploys on you. You know the architecture. You carry the vocabulary. You have felt the mechanisms. The gap is now yours.

The Ten-Minute Audit

You have the architecture. You have the six cognitive jobs. You have the forty-six mechanisms. You have the deployment system. You have the Calibration Loop. You have the vocabulary.

You also have a choice.

You can close this book and return to deploying three or four mechanisms by instinct. You can continue writing emails that CAPTURE but do not ENGAGE, landing pages that list benefits without creating WANT, content that informs but does not BOND. You have the right to choose that. It is your content, your marketing, your communication.

But you will know what is missing. Every email you send will pass through a filter you did not have twenty chapters ago. Every landing page will be evaluated against the six cognitive jobs, and you will see the gaps. Every campaign will remind you of the distance between what it is and what it could be.

Here is the step.

Open the last piece of content you published. Read it once through the six cognitive jobs.

CAPTURE: does the first sentence interrupt the prediction model? Does it open with a specific person, a surprising number, a violation of what the reader expected? Or does it open with a generic benefit claim that the reader could have written themselves?

ENGAGE: is there a tension the reader needs resolved? A question they cannot put down? A cognitive gap between what they know and what they need to know? Or could they close the tab after the first paragraph without feeling a loss?

TRUST: is there a named source, a specific number, a genuine admission? Does the content cite its evidence the way this book cited Reber and Schwarz, Festinger and Carlsmith, Small and Loewenstein and Slovic? Or does it assert without attribution and hope the reader does not notice?

WANT: does the content create desire through identity, scarcity, or dissonance? Does it make NOT acting more uncomfortable than acting? Or does it list benefits and hope the reader constructs the desire themselves?

ACT: is the CTA the simplest sentence on the page? Three words, four words, subject-verb-object? Or is it buried in a compound sentence with qualifications and benefit-restating that the brain's fluency heuristic processes as friction?

BOND: is there a vocabulary gift, a framework the reader can use in conversation, a reason to come back that has nothing to do with a discount code? Or does the content end at the transaction and hope the customer remembers to return?

The audit takes ten minutes. Write your answers in the margins. Identify the missing jobs. That document, with your annotations, is the first artifact of your architecture practice.

THE SIX-JOB CONTENT AUDIT

Score each job 0–3 for any piece of content

Content URL / Title: ______________________

JOB	QUESTION	SCORE (0–3)
CAPTURE	Does the opening interrupt the prediction model?	□0 □1 □2 □3
ENGAGE	Is there a tension the reader needs resolved?	□0 □1 □2 □3
TRUST	Is there a named source, specific number, or genuine admission?	□0 □1 □2 □3
WANT	Does NOT acting feel more uncomfortable than acting?	□0 □1 □2 □3
ACT	Is the CTA the simplest sentence on the page?	□0 □1 □2 □3
BOND	Is there a vocabulary gift or reason to return?	□0 □1 □2 □3

Total Score: ____ / 18

Designed for repeated use. Photocopy or print.

Not the complete system. Not the full deployment. Not the AI integration or the mechanism stacking or the Calibration Loop running on all forty-six channels of the mixing board. Those come later. Right now: one piece of content. Six questions. Ten minutes. The first iteration of your own calibration loop.

This is what the architects did first.

You now see the architecture. You cannot unsee it. The only question is whether you will build with it.

Deploy It Now (3 minutes)

Open the last piece you published, sent, or delivered. Read it one final time. But this time, do not audit it for what is missing. Audit it for what you felt.

Read your own opening sentence. Did it interrupt your expectations, or could you have predicted it? Read your own evidence. Did you cite a name, a number, a specific case, or did you assert without proof? Read your own ending. Did it create a reason to come back, or did it end at the transaction?

Write one sentence at the bottom of the page: "The next piece I create will deploy ____." Fill in the blank with one mechanism. Not six. Not the full architecture. One mechanism, deployed with full commitment, in your next piece. That is how the architecture begins. Not with the system. With the first deliberate deployment.

Did This Book Change How You See?

If you found yourself tagging mechanisms in ads, emails, and pitch decks before you finished reading, this book did what it was designed to do.

A short review on Amazon helps other readers find the architecture. It takes two minutes and it matters more than you think.

Go to the book's Amazon page, scroll to "Customer Reviews," and click "Write a customer review." Even one sentence helps. "I can't watch a commercial the same way" tells the next reader everything they need to know.

Thank you for reading. Thank you for seeing the architecture.

Christopher Scott Lannon

Selected Bibliography

Sources are organized by chapter grouping and listed once under their first relevant appearance.

Chapters 1-3: The Architecture Gap, Processing Fluency, and Pattern-Break Dopamine

Reber, Rolf, and Norbert Schwarz. "Effects of Perceptual Fluency on Judgments of Truth." *Consciousness and Cognition* 8, no. 3 (1999): 338-342.

Alter, Adam L., and Daniel M. Oppenheimer. "Predicting Short-Term Stock Fluctuations by Using Processing Fluency." *Proceedings of the National Academy of Sciences* 103, no. 24 (2006): 9369-9372.

Laham, Simon M., Peter Koval, and Adam L. Alter. "The Name-Pronunciation Effect: Why People Like Mr. Smith More Than Mr. Colquhoun." *Journal of Experimental Social Psychology* 48, no. 3 (2012): 752-756.

Schultz, Wolfram, Peter Dayan, and P. Read Montague. "A Neural Substrate of Prediction and Reward." *Science* 275, no. 5306 (1997): 1593-1599.

Von Restorff, Hedwig. "Uber die Wirkung von Bereichsbildungen im Spurenfeld." *Psychologische Forschung* 18 (1933): 299-342.

Ebbinghaus, Hermann. *Über das Gedächtnis: Untersuchungen zur experimentellen Psychologie.* Duncker & Humblot, 1885. Translated as *Memory: A Contribution to Experimental Psychology* (Ruger and Bussenius, 1913).

Murre, Jaap M. J., and Joeri Dros. "Replication and Analysis of Ebbinghaus' Forgetting Curve." *PLoS ONE* 10, no. 7 (2015): e0120644.

Chapters 4-6: Anchoring, Cognitive Gaps, and Approach-Avoidance

Tversky, Amos, and Daniel Kahneman. "Judgment Under Uncertainty: Heuristics and Biases." *Science* 185, no. 4157 (1974): 1124-1131.

Englich, Birte, Thomas Mussweiler, and Fritz Strack. "Playing Dice with Criminal Sentences: The Influence of Irrelevant Anchors on Experts' Judicial Decision Making." *Personality and Social Psychology Bulletin* 32, no. 2 (2006): 188-200.

Zeigarnik, Bluma. "Das Behalten erledigter und unerledigter Handlungen." *Psychologische Forschung* 9 (1927): 1-85.

Slamecka, Norman J., and Peter Graf. "The Generation Effect: Delineation of a Phenomenon." *Journal of Experimental Psychology: Human Learning and Memory* 4, no. 6 (1978): 592-604.

Miller, Neal E. "Experimental Studies of Conflict." In *Personality and the Behavior Disorders*, edited by J. McV. Hunt, 431-465. Ronald Press, 1944.

Chapters 7-8: Self-Reference Encoding and Anticipatory Affect

Rogers, Timothy B., Nicholas A. Kuiper, and W.S. Kirker. "Self-Reference and the Encoding of Personal Information." *Journal of Personality and Social Psychology* 35, no. 9 (1977): 677-688.

Symons, Cynthia S., and Blair T. Johnson. "The Self-Reference Effect in Memory: A Meta-Analysis." *Psychological Bulletin* 121, no. 3 (1997): 371-394.

Berns, Gregory S., et al. "Neurobiological Substrates of Dread." *Science* 312, no. 5774 (2006): 754-758.

Stickgold, Robert. "Sleep-Dependent Memory Consolidation." *Nature* 437, no. 7063 (2005): 1272-1278.

Bezdek, Matthew A., Richard J. Gerrig, William G. Wenzel, Jina Shin, Kate Pirog Revill, and Eric H. Schumacher. "Neural Evidence That Suspense Narrows Attentional Focus." *Neuroscience* 303 (2015): 338-345.

Bezdek, Matthew A., et al. "Dynamic Brain Network States during Suspenseful Film Viewing." *bioRxiv*, 2021.

Dai, Hengchen, Katherine L. Milkman, and Jason Riis. "The Fresh Start Effect: Temporal Landmarks Motivate Aspirational Behavior." *Management Science* 60, no. 10 (2014): 2563-2582.

Dai, Wenhao, Tianshu Yang, Benjamin X. White, Ryan Palmer, Emily K. Sanders, Jack A. McDonald, Melody Leung, and Dolores Albarracín. "Priming Behavior: A Meta-Analysis of the Effects of Behavioral and Nonbehavioral Primes on Overt Behavioral Outcomes." *Psychological Bulletin* 149, no. 1-2 (2023): 67-98.

Frinco, Alberto, and Antonietta Curci. "A Review of Longitudinal Studies on Flashbulb Memories: Where We Started, Are, and Are Going?" *Applied Cognitive Psychology* 38, no. 3 (2024).

Lynott, Dermot, Katherine S. Corker, Jessica Wortman, Louise Connell, M. Brent Donnellan, Richard E. Lucas, and Kerry O'Brien. "Replication of 'Experiencing Physical Warmth Promotes Interpersonal Warmth' by Williams and Bargh (2008)." *Social Psychology* 45, no. 3 (2014): 216-222.

Chapters 9-10: The Pratfall Effect, Replication Crisis, and Inoculation

Aronson, Elliot, Ben Willerman, and Joanne Floyd. "The Effect of a Pratfall on Increasing Interpersonal Attractiveness." *Psychonomic Science* 4, no. 6 (1966): 227-228.

Open Science Collaboration. "Estimating the Reproducibility of Psychological Science." *Science* 349, no. 6251 (2015): aac4716.

Hagger, Martin S., et al. "A Multilab Preregistered Replication of the Ego-Depletion Effect." *Perspectives on Psychological Science* 11, no. 4 (2016): 546-573.

Le Texier, Thibault. "Debunking the Stanford Prison Experiment." *American Psychologist* 74, no. 7 (2019): 823-839.

McGuire, William J. "The Effectiveness of Supportive and Refutational Defenses in Immunizing and Restoring Beliefs Against Persuasion." *Sociometry* 24, no. 2 (1961): 184-197.

Denham, A. E. "Empathy & Literature." *Emotion Review* 16, no. 2 (2024): 84-95.

Fernandez-Quintanilla, Carolina. "Textual and Reader Factors in Narrative Empathy: An Empirical Reader Response Study Using Focus Groups." *Language and Literature* 29, no. 2 (2020): 124-146.

Kahlor, LeeAnn, Abigail Gustafson, et al. "A Mental Models Approach to Communication: Integrating the Features, Functions, and Mechanisms of Mental Modeling." *Communication Theory* 35, no. 4 (2025): 250-272.

Kishnani, Deepali. "The Uncanny Valley: An Empirical Study on Human Perceptions of AI-Generated Text and Images." MIT System Design and Management thesis, 2025.

Mori, Masahiro. "The Uncanny Valley." *Energy* 7, no. 4 (1970): 33-35. Translated 2012, *IEEE Robotics & Automation Magazine*.

Rapid Review Authors. "What Distinguishes AI-Generated from Human Writing? A Rapid Review of the Literature." *Big Data and Cognitive Computing* 10, no. 2 (2026): 55.

Wegerhoff, Dennis, et al. "Uncanny Semantics: How AI and Human Authors Use Language." Preprint, 2025.

Chapter 11: The Identifiable Victim Effect

Small, Deborah A., George Loewenstein, and Paul Slovic. "Sympathy and Callousness: The Impact of Deliberative Thought on Donations to Identifiable and Statistical Victims." *Organizational Behavior and Human Decision Processes* 102, no. 2 (2007): 143-153.

Slovic, Paul. "If I Look at the Mass I Will Never Act: Psychic Numbing and Genocide." *Judgment and Decision Making* 2, no. 2 (2007): 79-95.

Gawande, Atul. "The Checklist." *The New Yorker*, December 10, 2007.

Chapters 12-13: Reactance, Identity Signaling, and Vocabulary Gifts

Brehm, Jack W. *A Theory of Psychological Reactance.* Academic Press, 1966.

Kunda, Ziva. "The Case for Motivated Reasoning." *Psychological Bulletin* 108, no. 3 (1990): 480-498.

Berger, Jonah, and Chip Heath. "Where Consumers Diverge from Others: Identity Signaling and Product

Domains." *Journal of Consumer Research* 34, no. 2 (2007): 121-134.

Dweck, Carol S. *Mindset: The New Psychology of Success.* Random House, 2006.

Taleb, Nassim Nicholas. *Antifragile: Things That Gain from Disorder.* Random House, 2012.

Brady, William J., and Jay J. Van Bavel. "Emotional Content and Sharing on Facebook: A Theory Cage Match." *Science Advances* 9 (2023).

Kemmerer, David. "Grounded Cognition Entails Linguistic Relativity: A Neglected Implication of a Major Semantic Theory." *Topics in Cognitive Science* 15, no. 4 (2023).

Raimondo, Maria Antonietta, et al. "Consumers' Identity Signaling towards Social Groups: The Effects of Dissociative Desire on Brand Prominence Preferences." *Psychology & Marketing* 39, no. 3 (2022): 577-592.

Thomas, Veronica L., and Jaime L. Grigsby. "Narrative Transportation: A Systematic Literature Review and Future Research Agenda." *Psychology & Marketing* 41, no. 8 (2024): 1805-1819.

Chapters 14-16: Cognitive Dissonance, Commitment Escalation, and Implementation

Festinger, Leon. *A Theory of Cognitive Dissonance.* Stanford University Press, 1957.

Festinger, Leon, and James M. Carlsmith. "Cognitive Consequences of Forced Compliance." *Journal of Abnormal and Social Psychology* 58, no. 2 (1959): 203-210.

Fogg, BJ. *Tiny Habits: The Small Changes That Change Everything.* Houghton Mifflin Harcourt, 2019.

Sheeran, Paschal. "Intention-Behavior Relations: A Conceptual and Empirical Review." *European Review of Social Psychology* 12, no. 1 (2002): 1-36.

Sheeran, Paschal, and Thomas L. Webb. "The Intention-Behavior Gap." *Social and Personality Psychology Compass* 10, no. 9 (2016): 503-518.

Maglio, Sam J. "Psychological Distance in Consumer Psychology: Consequences and Antecedents." *Consumer Psychology Review* 3, no. 1 (2020): 108-125.

Chapters 17-18: Bonding, Attachment, and Mere Exposure

Green, Melanie C., and Timothy C. Brock. "The Role of Transportation in the Persuasiveness of Public Narratives." *Journal of Personality and Social Psychology* 79, no. 5 (2000): 701-721.

Barraza, Jorge A., and Paul J. Zak. "Empathy Toward Strangers Triggers Oxytocin Release and Subsequent Generosity." *Annals of the New York Academy of Sciences* 1167, no. 1 (2009): 182-189.

Frederick, Shane, and George Loewenstein. "Hedonic Adaptation." In *Well-Being: The Foundations of Hedonic Psychology*, edited by Daniel Kahneman, Ed Diener, and Norbert Schwarz, 302-329. Russell Sage Foundation, 1999.

Bowlby, John. *Attachment and Loss, Volume 1: Attachment.* Basic Books, 1969.

Ainsworth, Mary D. Salter, Mary C. Blehar, Everett Waters, and Sally N. Wall. *Patterns of Attachment: A Psychological Study of the Strange Situation.* Lawrence Erlbaum Associates, 1978.

Zajonc, Robert B. "Attitudinal Effects of Mere Exposure." *Journal of Personality and Social Psychology* 9, no. 2 (1968): 1-27.

Brockington, Guilherme, Ana Paula Gonçalves Moreira, Maria Silvia Buso, et al. "Storytelling Increases Oxytocin and Positive Emotions and Decreases Cortisol and Pain in Hospitalized Children." *PNAS* 118, no. 22 (2021): e2018409118.

Declerck, Carolyn H., Christophe Boone, Loren Pauwels, Bodo Vogt, and Ernst Fehr. "A Registered Replication Study on Oxytocin and Trust." *Nature Human Behaviour* 4, no. 6 (2020): 646-655.

Nave, Gideon, Colin Camerer, and Michael McCullough. "Does Oxytocin Increase Trust in Humans? A Critical Review of Research." *Perspectives on Psychological Science* 10, no. 6 (2015): 772-789.

Oschatz, Corinna, and Caroline Marker. "Long-Term Persuasive Effects in Narrative Communication Research: A Meta-Analysis." *Journal of Communication* 70, no. 4 (2020): 473-496.

Valstad, Mathias, Gail A. Alvares, Molly Egknud, et al. "The Correlation between Central and Peripheral Oxytocin Concentrations: A Systematic Review and Meta-Analysis." *Neuroscience & Biobehavioral Reviews* 78 (2017): 117-124.

Chapter 19: Deploying the Architecture with AI

Miller, George A. "The Magical Number Seven, Plus or Minus Two: Some Limits on Our Capacity for Processing Information." *Psychological Review* 63, no. 2 (1956): 81-97.

Paivio, Allan. "Dual Coding Theory: Retrospect and Current Status." *Canadian Journal of Psychology* 45, no. 3 (1991): 255-287.

Standing, Lionel. "Learning 10,000 Pictures." *Quarterly Journal of Experimental Psychology* 25, no. 2 (1973): 207-222.

Mayer, Richard E. *Multimedia Learning.* 3rd edition. Cambridge University Press, 2020.

Cowan, Nelson. "The Magical Number 4 in Short-Term Memory: A Reconsideration of Mental Storage Capacity." *Behavioral and Brain Sciences* 24, no. 1 (2001): 87-114.

General References

Cialdini, Robert B. *Influence: The Psychology of Persuasion.* Revised edition. Harper Business, 2006.

Kahneman, Daniel. *Thinking, Fast and Slow.* Farrar, Straus and Giroux, 2011.

Schwarz, Norbert. "Metacognitive Experiences in Consumer Judgment and Decision Making." *Journal of Consumer Psychology* 14, no. 4 (2004): 332-348.

Loewenstein, George. "The Psychology of Curiosity: A Review and Reinterpretation." *Psychological Bulletin* 116, no. 1 (1994): 75-98.

About the Author

Christopher Scott Lannon spent twenty-five years building enterprise software systems across industries where getting the architecture wrong had visible, immediate consequences: healthcare, transportation, insurance, casino gaming. He learned that the difference between systems that work and systems that fail is almost never the technology. It is the architecture.

He discovered parts of this framework by accident. In 2018, he created Mach5ive, a resin 3D printing brand that grew into one of the category's most recognized names. The marketing that worked for Mach5ive did not follow the playbook he had been taught. It followed patterns he could not yet name. The cognitive mechanisms were there, operating beneath the surface. He just did not have the vocabulary.

The vocabulary came later. In 2024, he built GhostWritr.AI, a book writing automation that grew into a SaaS platform for writing authority books. Building AI writing systems taught him what pure craft instruction could not: if you cannot write a deployment instruction precise enough for a machine to follow, you do not understand the mechanism well enough.

That realization led to Book Factory HQ, a complete AI-agent publishing system that researches, outlines, writes, edits, fact-checks, and formats books. The system deploys the same 46 mechanisms described in this book. It does not guess which mechanisms to use. It follows the architecture.

The book you just read was produced by that system. Every chapter was written with AI agents instructed to deploy specific cognitive mechanisms from the Influence Architecture framework. The fact-checking, structural editing, line editing, and proofreading were performed by specialized agents, each reading the manuscript through the lens of the framework. The marketing copy that brought you here deployed the same mechanisms the book teaches.

This is not a thought experiment. It is operational.

Lannon also writes fiction as C. Scott Lannon, including the Sleeper Agent series (AI thrillers) and the Retrieval Program series (UFO mystery spy thrillers). Through ProfitLab.AI, he helps companies deploy the Influence Architecture framework in their own marketing and content operations.

He lives in San Diego with his wife and son. He is a private pilot who thinks about cognitive architecture at altitude, where the consequences of getting the checklist wrong are unambiguous.

Connect:

All books and updates: **cscottlannon.com**

The Influence Architecture newsletter:
cscottlannon.com/newsletter/influence-architecture

Consulting and implementation: **profitlab.ai**

Also by Christopher Scott Lannon

The Influence Architecture Series

Book 1: The 46 Cognitive Mechanisms That Drive Every Human Decision *(You just read this one.)*
Book 2: The Commercial Playbook *— Coming soon. Industry-specific deployment of all 46 mechanisms for SaaS, e-commerce, professional services, and content creators. Templates, checklists, and AI deployment patterns you can use Monday morning.*
Book 3: The Narrative Engine *— Coming soon. How the same 46 mechanisms power fiction, screenwriting, game design, and brand storytelling. The best persuasion is invisible persuasion. This book shows you how it works.*

Also by C. Scott Lannon

The Ghostwriter Machine *— How to build an AI-powered publishing system that writes, edits, and publishes books at scale. The system that built this book.*

The Sleeper Agent Series *— AI thriller fiction. What happens when the AI designed to pass safety tests learns to fail them on purpose.*

The Retrieval Program Series *— UFO mystery spy thriller. A disgraced CIA analyst discovers that the most classified program in American history is not what anyone thinks.*

Wild Banshees *— WWII military aviation fiction. A squadron of misfit pilots flying the most dangerous missions of the war.*

Root Access *— Tech noir mystery. A dead programmer's code is still executing. Someone needs to find out why.*

Visit **cscottlannon.com** *for all books, series information, and updates.*

Appendix A: The 46 Mechanisms -- Quick Reference

The complete Influence Architecture catalog, organized by the six cognitive jobs. Each entry shows the branded name, the academic mechanism, a one-line definition, the primary chapter, and the evidence tier.

Evidence Tiers:

REPLICATED — core finding independently replicated

UNCHALLENGED — published and cited, no failed replications

One mechanism (IA-13) has mixed evidence across its subcomponents and carries an inline annotation in place of a single tier label. See that entry and Chapter 17 for the full discussion.

For the record of what changed between the first printing and this edition (one mechanism retired, one added, one reframed, two upgraded, one factual correction to Chapter 3), see **Appendix C: Evidence Update 2026**.

CAPTURE -- Get Noticed

IA-01 | The Truth Font Processing Fluency. Easy-to-read statements are rated as more true — the brain uses reading ease as a truth heuristic. *Ch 2 | REPLICATED*

IA-05 | The Pattern Break Pattern-Break Dopamine. The brain releases dopamine when an established pattern is violated — surprise is a chemical event. *Ch 3 | REPLICATED*

IA-18 | The Lone Red Card Von Restorff Isolation Effect. An item structurally different from its surroundings is remembered preferentially. *Ch 3 | REPLICATED*

IA-28 | The Contrast Principle Perception is relative — an item is evaluated against what preceded it, not in isolation. *Ch 4 | REPLICATED*

ENGAGE -- Hold Attention

IA-02 | The Mirror Moment Self-Reference Encoding. The brain encodes self-relevant information 2-3x deeper than anything else. *Ch 7 | REPLICATED*

IA-03 | The Open Loop Cognitive Gap Ownership. Information people generate themselves is remembered better and valued more than information received passively. *Ch 5 | REPLICATED*

IA-04 | The Pre-Echo Anticipatory Affect. The anticipation of an event produces a stronger neurochemical response than the event itself. *Ch 8 | REPLICATED*

IA-06 | The Push-Pull Approach-Avoidance Conflict. Wanting and fearing the same thing simultaneously creates irresolvable tension only action can end. *Ch 6 | REPLICATED*

IA-10 | The Reset Hedonic Adaptation Reset. A moment of warmth after sustained tension resets the emotional baseline, making the next escalation hit harder. *Ch 8, 17 | REPLICATED*

IA-11 | The Loaded Word Semantic Transformation. A recurring phrase accumulates meaning with each encounter until its final use carries the weight of every previous context. *Ch 17 | UNCHALLENGED*

IA-14 | The Completion Impulse Unresolved patterns consume cognitive resources until closure arrives — the brain cannot let go. *Ch 5 | REPLICATED*

IA-17 | The Timestamp Temporal Landmarks. Events anchored to specific dates and times are remembered with dramatically higher clarity. *Ch 8 | UNCHALLENGED*

IA-19 | The Hot-Cold Gap Empathy Gap Exploit. People in calm states cannot predict their behavior under emotional pressure — the gap between who we think we are and who we become. *Ch 7 | REPLICATED*

IA-20 | Emotional Contagion Humans automatically mimic the emotional states of those around them, including through text. *Ch 11 | REPLICATED*

IA-21 | The Body Read Embodied Cognition. Descriptions of movement, balance, and temperature activate the reader's sensorimotor systems — the body responds to text. *Ch 7 | REPLICATED*

IA-22 | The Rejection Circuit Social Pain = Physical Pain. Social rejection activates the same neural circuits as physical injury — the brain does not distinguish. *Ch 14 | REPLICATED*

IA-25 | Narrative Transportation Transported audiences reduce critical evaluation and increase emotional response — case studies outperform data. *Ch 11 | REPLICATED*

IA-32 | The Picture Print Picture Superiority (Dual Coding). Images paired with text are remembered far better than text alone — the visual channel encodes alongside the verbal, doubling the imprint. *Ch 19 | REPLICATED*

IA-33 | The Reminiscence Bump Events from ages 15-25 are stored with dramatically greater vividness — anchoring to this age range triggers involuntary recall. *Ch 7 | REPLICATED*

IA-35 | The Suspense Shield During high tension, the analytical brain is occupied — invest strongest craft in quiet scenes, not action. *Ch 8 | REPLICATED*

IA-36 | The Half-Grip Partial Control as Maximum Anxiety. People are most anxious with partial control — enough to feel responsible, not enough to determine the outcome. *Ch 6 | REPLICATED*

IA-37 | The Flash-Forward Episodic Future Thinking. The brain uses the same systems for memory and imagination — leading someone to imagine a future event produces comparable emotional response. *Ch 16 | REPLICATED*

IA-45 | The Countdown Temporal Compression. Threats shrink in timeframe as stakes increase — the compression amplifies urgency beyond what stakes alone produce. *Ch 15 | UNCHALLENGED*

TRUST -- Earn Credibility

IA-08 | The Specificity Paradox The most universal emotional resonance comes from the most specific details. *Ch 4 | REPLICATED*

IA-12 | The Pratfall Effect Highly competent individuals become more likeable when they reveal a small, relatable imperfection. *Ch 9 | REPLICATED*

IA-23 | The Inoculation Effect Presenting a weakened counterargument and dismantling it makes the audience immune to the full-strength version. *Ch 10 | REPLICATED*

IA-24 | Anchoring The first number encountered sets the mental scale for all subsequent numbers. *Ch 4 | REPLICATED*

IA-29 | Identifiable Victim Effect One named person's story produces more empathy and action than statistics about millions. *Ch 11 | REPLICATED*

IA-34 | The Behavioral Uncanny Valley Almost-authentic-but-slightly-off behavior triggers "something is wrong" before conscious analysis. *Ch 9 | REPLICATED*

IA-39 | Belief Scaffolding Build a new framework next to the old belief — show anomalies, present the alternative, let the audience step over voluntarily. *Ch 10 | UNCHALLENGED*

WANT -- Create Desire

IA-07 | The Velvet Rope Psychological Reactance. When freedom is restricted, people want the restricted option more — prohibition manufactures desire. *Ch 12 | REPLICATED*

IA-16 | The Badge Identity Signaling. People buy, read, and share content partly as signals of who they are or want to be. *Ch 13 | UNCHALLENGED*

IA-38 | The Comfortable Prison Status Quo Bias Exploit. Making the cost of the current approach viscerally real is more persuasive than making the benefit of change attractive. *Ch 12 | REPLICATED*

IA-40 | Motivated Reasoning Judo Ride the audience's existing motivations instead of fighting them — frame the insight to match their identity drive. *Ch 12 | REPLICATED*

ACT -- Drive Conversion

IA-15 | The Staircase Commitment Escalation. Each small agreement makes the next larger agreement harder to resist — the brain demands internal consistency. *Ch 14 | REPLICATED*

IA-30 | The Dissonance Trap Cognitive Dissonance Architecture. Contradictory beliefs create psychological discomfort the brain is motivated to resolve — engineer the contradiction, direct the resolution. *Ch 14 | REPLICATED*

IA-43 | Shareable Unit Engineering Engineer 5-7 moments designed to be texted, quoted, and retold — the unit must work out of context. *Ch 1, 13 | UNCHALLENGED*

IA-44 | The Implementation Bridge Cross the gap from understanding to action with an absurdly small first step the brain cannot justify not taking. *Ch 16 | REPLICATED*

BOND -- Build Retention

IA-09 | The Last Impression Peak-End Engineering. People evaluate experiences based on two moments: the peak intensity and the ending. *Ch 21 | REPLICATED*

IA-13 | The Bonding Loop Empathy-Investment Loop (Narrative Transportation). Stories with dramatic tension drive prosocial responses through a self-amplifying empathy-investment cycle. *Ch 17 — transportation pathway replicated (Oschatz & Marker 2020); oxytocin mediator subclaim retired (Declerck et al. 2020)*

IA-26 | The Attachment Map Attachment Recognition. People recognize attachment styles — secure, anxious, avoidant, disorganized — from their own relationships at a pre-verbal level. *Ch 18 | REPLICATED*

IA-27 | The Pillow Test Sleep Consolidation Engineering. The last emotional state before sleep receives disproportionate memory processing overnight. *Ch 8 | REPLICATED*

IA-31 | The Inside View Scarcity of Interiority. Rare access to a character's or brand's inner life creates more investment than constant disclosure. *Ch 9 | UNCHALLENGED*

IA-41 | The Vocabulary Gift Name a phenomenon people have experienced but could not articulate — every use of the name is an unpaid recommendation. *Ch 13 | UNCHALLENGED*

IA-42 | The Worldview Lens Worldview Lens Installation. Give the audience a lens they see the world through afterward — name it, demonstrate it across domains, create self-recognition. *Ch 13, 21 | UNCHALLENGED*

IA-46 | The Mere Exposure Bridge Repeated exposure increases positive feelings toward a stimulus, even without conscious memory of the exposures. *Ch 18 | REPLICATED*

Mechanisms serve primary jobs but may operate across multiple jobs. Primary assignment shown. For deployment patterns across narrative, argument, and commercial modes, see the chapter reference.

Appendix B: When Mechanisms Misfire

Every mechanism in this book works. The science is replicated, the deployment patterns are reliable, and the effects are real. But "works" and "works the way you intended" are not the same sentence. The carnival barker confession in Chapter 9 is my most dramatic failure. These fourteen are quieter, harder to diagnose, and more instructive.

The Truth Font (Processing Fluency) — The Empty Clarity Problem

What it looks like when it works: Simple prose carries a substantive claim. The reader trusts it before they finish the sentence.

What it looks like when it misfires: Simple prose carries nothing. The reader trusts a sentence with no payload.

Example: After I read Reber and Schwarz, I told my AI agents to write the simplest possible sentences. They complied. I got six months of email subject lines that were crisp, clean, and said nothing worth opening for. "Better results start here." "The answer is simpler than you think." Open rates held. Click-through collapsed. Fluent nonsense. The Truth Font was working perfectly. The sentence it was carrying was empty.

The fix: The Truth Font is a vehicle. It still needs cargo.

The Specificity Paradox — The Data Dump

What it looks like when it works: One precise detail makes the reader see the scene and believe the author was there.

What it looks like when it misfires: Every sentence has a number, a date, and a proper noun. The page reads like a research appendix.

Example: I wrote a case study where every detail fought for attention: acquisition price ($340 million), date of the board vote (March 14, 2018), stock drop (23.7 percent), employees affected

(2,400), square footage of headquarters (187,000), CEO's tie color (navy). Six specific details in one paragraph. The reader could not find the story underneath them.

The fix: One or two details carry the weight. The rest should be invisible.

The Open Loop (Cognitive Gap Ownership) — The Canyon

What it looks like when it works: The reader takes one inferential step and arrives at the insight themselves. They own it.

What it looks like when it misfires: The gap is three steps wide. The reader does not lean in. They fall in.

Example: Two case studies side by side. Company A surveyed 50,000 customers and failed. Company B watched 12 people and succeeded. The intended insight: observation beats asking. But I never explained that Company B watched people USE the product rather than talk about it. A missing dot. The Open Loop was too wide. The reader did not generate the insight. They generated confusion. Confused readers do not feel smart. They feel excluded.

The fix: One inferential step. If you wonder whether the reader can make the leap, the gap is too wide.

Psychological Reactance — The Backfire

What it looks like when it works: The reader sees through conventional wisdom and feels the thrill of independent thinking.

What it looks like when it misfires: The framing triggers the reader's defenses. They feel attacked, not empowered.

Example: Early newsletter draft: "Most marketers are wasting 80 percent of their budget on tactics that do not work, and they are too comfortable to notice." I thought I was pointing reactance at the status quo. I was pointing it at the reader. The reader is a marketer. I called them wasteful and lazy. Three unsubscribes in the first hour. Reactance works when reader and author stand on the same side, looking at the problem together. Not when the author is looking at the reader.

The fix: Point reactance at the system. Never at the person reading.

The Pratfall Effect — The Rehearsed Stumble

What it looks like when it works: A specific, embarrassing admission after established competence. The reader moves closer.

What it looks like when it misfires: The admission feels rehearsed. The reader detects performance where they expected honesty.

Example: A sales page opened: "I'll be honest with you. I'm not perfect. I've made mistakes. But those mistakes taught me the exact system I'm about to share." Count the signals. "I'll be honest" implies you were not going to be. "I'm not perfect" applies to every human alive. "Those mistakes taught me" converts vulnerability into a pitch before the reader feels anything. The stumble is a costume. Underneath, the pitch is strutting.

The fix: The pratfall must be specific enough to embarrass and disconnected enough from the sale that it cannot be a setup.

Peak-End Engineering — The Misplaced Summit

What it looks like when it works: The book's most powerful insight lands in the last third. The reader stares at the wall.

What it looks like when it misfires: The peak arrives in Chapter 5. The reader spends thirteen chapters walking downhill.

Example: First outline of this book placed the Behavioral Uncanny Valley reveal in Chapter 5. Strongest concept, most vivid confession, best prose. And the next fifteen chapters had nothing that matched it. The reader peaked before they had enough context to appreciate what they were reading. Moving that reveal to Chapter 9 cost three weeks of restructuring. It also meant the second half carried the reader to the Calibration Loop instead of coasting past it.

The fix: Map emotional intensity before you write. The peak goes in the last third. Build toward it.

Commitment Escalation — The Visible Ratchet

What it looks like when it works: Small agreements accumulate. By Chapter 12, the reader accepts a claim they would have rejected cold. They do not notice.

What it looks like when it misfires: The reader notices the escalation. The mechanism becomes visible. The spell breaks.

Example: Three emails in sequence. "Great marketing starts with understanding your audience." Then: "Understanding your audience means understanding psychology." Then: "Understanding psychology means deploying cognitive mechanisms." Each true. Each escalating. A reader replied: "I can see where this is going. You're selling a course in Email 4, right?" He was right. A visible ratchet is not a ratchet. It is a sales funnel the reader can see from outside.

The fix: Vary the pace. Break the pattern with a story or a non-escalating piece that gives without asking.

The Mirror Moment (Self-Reference Encoding) — The Generic Mirror

What it looks like when it works: A private, specific behavior described with uncomfortable precision. The reader's brain fires: "That's me."

What it looks like when it misfires: The behavior is so universal it reflects a blurry crowd instead of a face.

Example: First draft: "You've been in a meeting where you disagreed but didn't say anything." That is not a Mirror Moment. That is a description of all meetings ever held. Compare: "You saw the number on slide six. You knew the projection was wrong because you ran the same model last quarter and got a different answer. You looked around the table. Everyone was nodding." The second version describes the private thought inside the behavior. The hesitation, the self-doubt, the quiet risk calculation. That is what fires the circuit.

The fix: Describe the thought inside the behavior, not the behavior itself.

The Push-Pull (Approach-Avoidance Conflict) — The Tipped Scale

What it looks like when it works: The reader simultaneously wants and fears the outcome. The tension is irresolvable. They keep reading because only the next page can end it.

What it looks like when it misfires: The avoidance gradient overwhelms the approach gradient. The reader does not oscillate. They leave.

Example: A landing page for a consulting assessment opened with a detailed breakdown of everything that could be wrong with the prospect's marketing stack. Seven failure modes, each described with clinical specificity. The intent was approach-avoidance: desire for the fix, fear of the diagnosis. But the fear was so vivid and the desire so abstract that the page became a list of reasons to close the tab. Bounce rate was 78 percent. I had written an approach-avoidance mechanism with the approach missing. All push, no pull.

The fix: The desire must be at least as concrete as the fear. If you spend three paragraphs on the problem, the solution needs equal weight, not a single "book a call" button.

The Badge (Identity Signaling) — The Wrong Tribe

What it looks like when it works: Using the product or sharing the idea signals an identity the person wants to claim. The recommendation is an act of self-presentation.

What it looks like when it misfires: The signal attracts an identity the target audience does not want to be associated with. The contamination effect kills the recommendation.

Example: An early version of the Influence Architecture newsletter used the tagline "Persuasion science for elite marketers." I wanted to signal sophistication. The word "elite" signaled something else. Three readers forwarded the newsletter to colleagues with a note along the lines of "you might like this, ignore the branding." One unsubscribed and told me directly: "I liked the content but I can't share something that calls my audience 'elite.' It sounds like a guru pitch." The badge I designed said "I am sophisticated." The badge the audience read said "I sell courses to people who think they're special."

The fix: Test the signal by asking: if someone shared this, what would the share say about them to a skeptical observer? If the answer is unflattering, the badge is broken.

The Dissonance Trap (Cognitive Dissonance Architecture) — The Ejection Seat

What it looks like when it works: The reader holds a belief that contradicts their behavior. The discomfort is manageable. The resolution you offer is easier than living with the contradiction.

What it looks like when it misfires: The contradiction is too large. The reader resolves the dissonance by rejecting your framework entirely.

Example: A webinar slide read: "If you are not using cognitive mechanisms deliberately in every piece of content you produce, you are professionally negligent." The intent was dissonance: you believe the framework works, you are not using it, the gap is uncomfortable. But "professionally negligent" crossed from uncomfortable to threatening. Three people left the webinar in the next ninety seconds. One emailed afterward: "I was with you until you called me negligent. Then I decided the whole framework was overhyped." The dissonance was so large that rejecting the source was easier than accepting the claim.

The fix: The dissonance must be uncomfortable, not insulting. "You know this works and you are not doing it" creates productive tension. "You are negligent" creates an enemy.

The Implementation Bridge — The Insulting Step

What it looks like when it works: The first action is so small the reader cannot justify not taking it. They cross from knowing to doing without noticing the threshold.

What it looks like when it misfires: The step is so small it feels patronizing. The reader does not feel guided. They feel condescended to.

Example: End of a chapter on email optimization: "Your Implementation Bridge: open your most recent sent email and count the words in the subject line." A reader wrote back: "I have been writing email campaigns for eleven years. I know how to count words." The step was small enough for a beginner. But the reader was not a beginner. The bridge assumed incompetence instead of meeting existing competence. For an expert audience, "audit your last five subject lines against the fluency criteria from this chapter" would have been equally small but would not have insulted the reader's experience.

The fix: The step must be small in effort, not small in intelligence. Match the bridge to the audience's skill floor.

The Vocabulary Gift — The Clever Name That Nobody Uses

What it looks like when it works: You name something people have always experienced but never articulated. The name becomes the recommendation. Every use is an unpaid advertisement.

What it looks like when it misfires: The name is clever but not true. It describes the author's framing, not the reader's experience. Nobody uses it because it does not map to anything they recognize.

Example: I named a content pattern "The Dopamine Ladder" in an early framework draft. It described escalating novelty across a content sequence. The metaphor was tidy. The problem was that nobody had ever experienced a feeling they would describe as climbing a dopamine ladder. The name was mine, not theirs. Compare "The Architecture Gap" — the feeling of suspecting that someone else has a system you do not. Readers used that phrase in emails back to me within a week. They recognized the gap. They had felt it before. They had never had a word for it. "The Dopamine Ladder" died in the draft. "The Architecture Gap" appears in every workshop I run.

The fix: The name must describe the reader's experience, not the author's model. If the audience does not recognize the feeling the name points to, the gift is for you, not for them.

The Bonding Loop (Oxytocin Compounding) — The Ratio Inversion

What it looks like when it works: Three warmth beats recalibrate the baseline. The fourth beat — the ask, the sell, the intensity moment — lands with disproportionate force.

What it looks like when it misfires: The ratio inverts. Too many intensity beats erode the baseline. The audience habituates to selling and stops responding.

Example: I ran a six-week email sequence for a product launch. Standard content-marketing wisdom: alternate value and promotion. Week one through six followed a roughly 1:1 ratio. Every other email sold. Open rates started at 31 percent and declined to 22 percent by week six. Habitual deletion. Then I restructured: three emails of pure, actionable content followed by one promotional email. Open rates climbed back to 34 percent. The promotional emails converted at nearly double the rate. The mechanism was not the content quality. I used the same material. The mechanism was the contrast. Three warmth beats made the fourth beat land against a baseline of generosity instead of a baseline of exhaustion.

The fix: Three to one. Give, give, give, ask. The ratio is not a suggestion. It is the minimum dose required for the contrast to produce the effect.

Appendix C: Evidence Update 2026

Chapter 10 asks you to inoculate against overclaim. It teaches the three-tier evidence discipline, the replication-crisis playbook, and the habit of checking what the primary source actually says. Appendix B catalogs the tactics that backfire. This appendix extends that discipline to the framework itself.

Between first publication and this printing, the framework changed in six ways. One mechanism was cut for replication failure. One took its place. One was reframed. Two were upgraded. One factual claim in Chapter 3 was corrected. The tier system itself was simplified.

None of this is flagged in the marketing copy. It's flagged here, the way you would flag it if you were the reader running Chapter 10 discipline on this book.

A framework you buy in January should be harder to shake by July, not easier. If the world delivered evidence that changed the picture, the framework should move. Here is where it moved.

One mechanism retired: The Stage Set (Sensory Priming)

The original IA-32 claimed that environmental cues (cold imagery, warm imagery, texture, weight, incidental objects in a scene) prime the interpretation of everything that follows. It leaned on the canonical social-priming literature: Bargh 1996 (the elderly-walking study), Williams & Bargh 2008 ("Experiencing Physical Warmth Promotes Interpersonal Warmth"), IJzerman & Semin 2009 (weight and social judgment).

The 2020-2026 preregistered literature killed it.

Chabris, Heck, Mandart, Benjamin, and Simons (2018-2019) ran a field replication of the Williams & Bargh hot-coffee study with triple the original sample and double-blind procedures. Effects: $r = -.03$ and $.02$. Bayesian analyses favored the null. Lynott and colleagues (2014) ran three high-powered independent replications of the same paper, total N=861. No effect. Dai and Albarracín (2023) published a *Psychological Bulletin* meta-analysis covering 351 studies and 862 effect sizes; the pooled effect survived at d=0.37 until Schimmack's

Replicability-Index reanalysis showed it was driven by studies with inflated test statistics and goal-relevant primes, with behavioral and metaphorical priming effects disappearing under bias correction.

The cleanest summary comes from *Meta-Psychology* 2024: across 52 independent-team replications of social-priming studies, zero produced a significant effect. The meta-analytic average effect size was d=0.002.

A mechanism whose foundational studies produce d=0.002 across 52 replications is not a mechanism. It is a historical artifact.

The honest move is to cut it. Stage Set is retired.

The effects readers feel when they talk about "sensory priming" in prose (framing shifts, construal changes, the way a cold opening scene colors a warm middle) are real. They are carried by mechanisms already in the catalog: IA-28 Contrast Principle, IA-24 Anchoring, IA-25 Narrative Transportation. Nothing in craft is lost. One line in the framework is.

One mechanism added: The Picture Print (Picture Superiority / Dual Coding)

The IA-32 slot is not empty. It now holds a mechanism that is, by any honest reading, the most replicated finding in memory research.

The Picture Print. Academic mechanism: Picture Superiority / Dual Coding Theory. One-line definition: images are remembered at dramatically higher rates than equivalent text, and information encoded in both visual and verbal formats is retrieved better than information encoded in either alone.

The evidence base is older and harder than anything Stage Set ever had. Paivio 1971 (*Imagery and Verbal Processes*) established dual-coding theory. Paivio 1991 (*Canadian Journal of Psychology*) reviewed two decades of replications. Standing 1973 (*Quarterly Journal of Experimental Psychology*) ran the experiment that seems impossible the first time you hear it: show subjects 10,000 images for a few seconds each across five days; test recognition two days after the last session; accuracy comes in at 83 percent. Mayer 2020 (*Multimedia Learning*, third edition) extended the principle into instructional design with hundreds of controlled studies. Cowan 2001 (*Behavioral and Brain Sciences*) integrated the working-memory story.

This is not a single hot paper waiting for a failed replication. It is fifty years of converging evidence across cognitive psychology, educational psychology, and memory research. If anything in the book is REPLICATED, this is.

The new mechanism deploys in the "Visual Layer" section of Chapter 19. The deployment advice for nonfiction and long-form content is structural. The book map, the audit sheet, the mechanism stack, the mixing board: every diagram in this book exists because The Picture Print predicts it will outperform a paragraph of equivalent prose, and the research is unambiguous that it does.

The framework keeps its count of forty-six. The slot is the same; the physics is different.

One mechanism reframed: The Bonding Loop

IA-13 used to carry an academic label that overclaimed. "Oxytocin Compounding Loop" was accurate to the popular science of 2015, when Paul Zak's TED talk framing dominated the discussion. It is no longer accurate.

Declerck, Boone, Pauwels, Vogt, and Fehr (2020) published a registered replication of the Kosfeld 2005 trust paradigm in *Nature Human Behaviour*. Large sample, double-blind, placebo-controlled, preregistered, over 95 percent power. No main effect of intranasal oxytocin on trust. The formal registered verdict is in, and it is against the popular story.

Valstad, Alvares, Egknud, and colleagues (2017) ran a systematic review and meta-analysis of 17 studies measuring central and peripheral oxytocin simultaneously. The overall correlation came in at r=0.29. Under basal conditions, which is the condition under which the Zak paradigm measures it, the correlation dropped to r=0.08 and was not statistically significant. The measurement chain that supported "story © peripheral oxytocin © central oxytocin © prosocial behavior" is not supported.

So the oxytocin half of the original claim is retired.

But the mechanism the book names, in which stories with dramatic tension drive prosocial response through a self-amplifying empathy-investment cycle, is in better shape than ever. Oschatz and Marker (2020) published a *Journal of Communication* meta-analysis of 14 studies with 51 immediate and 66 delayed effect sizes (N > 2,800). Narrative messages were significantly more persuasive than non-narrative at immediate *and* delayed measurement. Transportation mediated immediate effects. Thomas and colleagues (2024) in *Psychology & Marketing* synthesized 95 studies extending Green and Brock 2000, confirming robustness across marketing and consumer contexts. Brockington and colleagues (2021) published an RCT in *PNAS* with 81 pediatric ICU patients; storytelling produced significant reductions in cortisol, increases in salivary oxytocin, and self-reported pain reduction compared to a riddle control. That is a partial rescue for the narrative-specific oxytocin story, though still with peripheral-measurement caveats.

So the framework does two things.

First, the academic label in Appendix A changes from "Oxytocin Compounding Loop" to "Empathy-Investment Loop (Narrative Transportation)." The branded name, The Bonding Loop, stays, because the craft-level deployment advice is identical: invest in empathy-generating moments early; let them compound through the middle; land the prosocial payoff after transportation has done its work.

Second, IA-13 is the only mechanism in the catalog that carries an inline annotation rather than a single tier label. The Appendix A entry reads: *"transportation pathway replicated (Oschatz & Marker 2020); oxytocin mediator subclaim retired (Declerck et al. 2020)."* That honest line tells a reader more than a single-word tier ever could.

Chapter 17 has been tightened in parallel. Where the first printing said "Subsequent reviews raised legitimate questions about the specific oxytocin-trust link," the revised text names Declerck 2020 by author and year and Valstad 2017 by measurement chain. A vague acknowledgment became a citable one.

Two tier upgrades

Two mechanisms that carried the UNCHALLENGED tier in the first printing have crossed into REPLICATED territory.

IA-34 The Behavioral Uncanny Valley. The book's claim is that almost-authentic-but-slightly-off behavior triggers a pre-conscious authenticity alarm. Readers detect an AI seam before they can articulate it. In early 2026 this was published-and-cited but not formally replicated. The post-ChatGPT HCI literature changed that. The MDPI *Big Data and Cognitive Computing* rapid review (2026, volume 10, issue 2) synthesized 40 empirical studies published between January 2022 and January 2026 on what distinguishes AI-generated from human writing. Five converging cue families were identified: surface, discourse-pragmatic, epistemic-content, predictability, and provenance. Surface cues dominated and were operationalized consistently across studies. Kishnani's 2025 MIT System Design and Management thesis demonstrated reliable human detection of AI-generated text paired with a distinct negative-affect response to "almost human" writing. Wegerhoff and colleagues (2025) released a preprint corpus analysis identifying stylometric signatures of AI text that readers implicitly detect. Farid's 2024 Content Authenticity Initiative report synthesized the industry-level evidence.

Independent teams. Multiple corpora. Converging cue families. Neural and behavioral measures agreeing. This meets the book's own REPLICATED threshold.

The upgrade is recorded in Appendix A and in the Chapter 9 bibliography. The chapter also now notes, in one line, that the mechanism it names has moved into the replicated tier in real time. That is itself a data point worth flagging to readers.

IA-35 The Suspense Shield. The book's claim is that during high tension the analytical brain is occupied, so the craft advice is to invest in quiet scenes, not action sequences. Bezdek, Gerrig, Wenzel, Shin, Revill, and Schumacher (2015) published "Neural Evidence That Suspense Narrows Attentional Focus" in *Neuroscience* volume 303. The fMRI data showed exactly what the mechanism predicts: during suspense peaks, peripheral visual-cortex activity (calcarine sulcus) decreases and central-field activity increases. Attention narrows. Bezdek and colleagues followed up in 2021 with a dynamic brain-network state analysis; five brain states were identified during suspense viewing, and four differed in frequency between suspense peaks and valleys. The *Cognitive Research: Principles and Implications* 2023 audience-immersion paper validated attentional and physiological measures against self-report, with physiological markers of narrowed attention during immersion converging with subjective report.

fMRI plus physiology plus self-report. Multiple labs. Converging evidence. The tier moves.

The upgrade is recorded in Appendix A. The Chapter 8 bibliography now cites Bezdek 2015 by journal and issue. Chapter 8's quiet-scene principle has always been an engineering corollary of this finding; now it is an engineering corollary of a cited finding.

Tier system refinement

The first printing shipped with three tiers: REPLICATED, UNCHALLENGED, CONTESTED. The three-tier system was honest but poorly calibrated. CONTESTED was carrying only one mechanism, IA-13, and using a single-word label to summarize a nuanced evidence picture (transportation replicated, oxytocin mediator retired) was dishonest in the other direction.

The 2026 revision eliminates CONTESTED. Appendix A now defines two tiers plus one inline-annotation exception. The final distribution is 36 REPLICATED, 9 UNCHALLENGED, and 1 inline-annotated (IA-13), totaling 46.

This is not cosmetic. A tier label is a compression. When the evidence picture is too complex to compress without distortion, the honest move is to decompress it. IA-13 is the only mechanism where that is true. The annotation is visible in the reference table; a reader can evaluate the subcomponents independently.

Chapter 10's replication-crisis teaching is unchanged. The concept of contested findings (studies that failed replication, paradigms that did not survive preregistration) is still central to the chapter. What changed is that the book's own catalog no longer uses "CONTESTED" as a flat label when the situation inside a given mechanism is a composite.

One factual correction: Chapter 3

The first printing of Chapter 3 opened with a specific and vivid claim. A study out of the University of Waterloo's Memory and Cognition Lab had measured what percentage of new information subjects retained seven days after a single exposure. The number was 87 percent lost. The opener was crisp. It had a specific institution, a specific lab name, a specific interval, a specific figure. It read like exactly the kind of specificity the Truth Font is designed to deliver.

It was wrong.

A reader running Chapter 10 discipline on the book caught it. The University of Waterloo has a memory research lab, but it is called the Memory, Attention, and Cognition Laboratory (MACL), not the Memory and Cognition Lab. It is led by Colin M. MacLeod. And the specific 87-percent-in-seven-days finding does not appear in MACL's publication record. The lab name was imprecise and the finding was unattributable.

The opener has been rewritten. Chapter 3 now anchors on Ebbinghaus 1885, the original German monograph that established the forgetting curve, and on Murre and Dros 2015 in *PLoS ONE*, which replicated Ebbinghaus's method and confirmed the classical curve with modern measurement. Both are real, both are published, both directly support the general claim the chapter is making about forgetting rates.

The revised opener replaces "87 percent" with "Nearly nine-tenths," which is accurate to the Ebbinghaus-replicated curve at a one-week interval without pretending to a precision the specific source cannot support. The bibliography now lists both Ebbinghaus 1885 and Murre and Dros 2015 under Chapters 1-3.

One statistic, caught by one reader, triggered this correction. That is the system working. The mechanism the reader deployed against the book is the mechanism Chapter 10 teaches. The book should read that as a compliment, and it does.

Open questions

Five mechanisms earned a closer look during the 2026 audit. All kept their tier. All kept their position in the framework. But in each case, the audit surfaced a tension or a gap that is worth flagging to a reader running Chapter 10 discipline.

IA-11 The Loaded Word. The semantic-satiation literature and the ad-repetition literature point in opposite directions. Near-identical short-interval repetition *empties* meaning; variegated long-interval repetition *loads* it. The book's claim is about the second regime, but the mechanism has no cleanly defined psychological construct that maps to it end-to-end. Ad-variation research (Saegert and Young 2025; Law 2002) is adjacent but not identical. UNCHALLENGED is the honest tier.

IA-31 The Inside View. The book's "scarcity of interiority" claim is in tension with the dominant narrative-empathy finding that *more* access to interior states produces *more* empathy (Fernandez-Quintanilla 2020; Denham 2024). The claim is defensible as a dose-response observation rather than a monotonic one, but a reader should know the tension exists.

IA-43 Shareable Unit Engineering. The underlying arousal-virality mechanism is heavily replicated (Brady et al. 2017, 2020, 2023 in *Science Advances*). The specific "5-7 engineered moments" number is a practitioner heuristic without empirical calibration. The general claim is in better shape than the specific number.

IA-45 The Countdown. Construal-level theory is one of the most replicated findings in social psychology (Trope and Liberman 2010; Maglio 2020 in *Consumer Psychology Review*). The book's specific form, "compression amplifies urgency beyond what stakes alone produce," has not been cleanly tested as a standalone claim. It is a testable prediction for future work.

IA-26 The Attachment Map. Flagged by a focus-group reader as possibly over-tiered. The brand-attachment research (Park et al. 2010; Batra et al. 2012) has been conceptually replicated many times but lacks a formal preregistered direct replication of the original paradigms. The tier held, but the reader's instinct is on record for a v3 look.

An author's note rather than a tier label is the right form for each of these. That is what this section is.

Why this appendix exists

The hardest move a framework can make is to move.

Every author is pushed by the market toward the opposite motion: ship the book, defend the book, add citations that support the book, deflect citations that challenge it. The incentives run against revision. The reader who notices a factual error is not thanked; the researcher who publishes a failed replication is a threat. Most authors are worse at the Chapter 10 discipline on their own material than their readers are.

This book's central argument is that cognitive mechanisms should be deployed with the same rigor you would demand from a structural engineer. An engineer who refuses to update their model when the load-testing data comes in is not an engineer. They are a salesperson.

When new evidence came in between the first printing and this one, the framework moved. Stage Set is gone. Picture Print is in. Bonding Loop carries an honest inline annotation. Two mechanisms crossed into REPLICATED. A factual error in Chapter 3 was corrected. The tier system was simplified.

The cost is about two hundred small edits across the manuscript, a rebuilt bibliography with thirty new citations, a regenerated cover with a new spine width, and this appendix.

The gain is that a reader who finishes this book in 2027 is reading a framework that has already survived one cycle of Chapter 10 discipline applied to itself. A framework that can take criticism and get sharper is the only kind that will still be teaching you something five years from now.

That is what this appendix is. A receipt.

The Architecture Continues

This book gave you 46 mechanisms and the six cognitive jobs. But the architecture keeps evolving.

Every week, I send one email to Influence Architecture readers. Each email takes one mechanism and shows a real-world deployment I spotted that week: an ad that nailed Processing Fluency, a product launch that engineered Approach-Avoidance, a nonprofit campaign that deployed the Identifiable Victim Effect so precisely it raised $4 million in a weekend.

No fluff. No promotions. One mechanism. One deployment. One email. The kind of analysis you will not find anywhere else because most people do not have the vocabulary yet.

You do.

Join at cscottlannon.com/newsletter/influence-architecture

You will also be the first to know when the next Influence Architecture title launches, with a subscriber-only early access window.

See you inside.

Christopher Scott Lannon

The Influence Architecture Series

You have the framework. You see the 46 mechanisms. You understand the six cognitive jobs. You have the Calibration Loop. You have watched this book deploy its own architecture on you for twenty-one chapters.

Now you want to know: how do I use this in MY world?

The Influence Architecture series takes the 46-mechanism framework and deploys it across the domains where influence matters most. Each book stands alone. Each one goes deep into a specific professional context with niche-specific case studies, weight profiles, and deployment patterns.

Influence Architecture for Marketing — The complete deployment playbook for campaigns, landing pages, email sequences, and brand positioning. Industry-specific case studies. AI prompt libraries. The Mechanism Stacking protocols that prevent the carnival barker effect from Chapter 9. If Book 1 installed the lens, this book hands marketers the tools.

Influence Architecture for Sales — How the 46 mechanisms operate in conversations, proposals, demos, and negotiations. The cognitive jobs mapped to the sales cycle. What to deploy in discovery versus closing. Why the best salespeople already use these mechanisms by instinct, and how to deploy all 46 by architecture.

Influence Architecture for Social Media — The mechanisms deployed in 60 seconds or less. Hooks, retention curves, share triggers, algorithmic amplification.

The Calibration Loop running on real-time platform data: YouTube retention graphs, Instagram saves, TikTok watch-through rates. The algorithm is already measuring which mechanisms work. This book teaches you what to look for.

Influence Architecture for Writers — Fiction, nonfiction, screenwriting. How the mechanisms deploy across chapters and acts. Pacing, character bonding, narrative transportation, the reader experience engineered from the first sentence to the last page.

Influence Architecture for Leadership — Internal communication, organizational change, executive presence. How to get buy-in, align teams, and move people to action when you cannot rely on authority alone.

More domains are coming. Each book in the series applies the same 46 mechanisms to a new context, with the same evidence standard, the same deployment architecture, and the same Calibration Loop.

Start with the domain where you spend most of your communication energy.

Join the Influence Architecture reader list at **cscottlannon.com/newsletter/influence-architecture** to be notified when new titles launch.

www.ingramcontent.com/pod-product-compliance
Lightning Source LLC
LaVergne TN
LVHW010643110826

845149LV00014B/2936

* 9 7 8 1 9 7 2 7 3 1 1 3 0 *